THE FINAL MISSION

Printed in the United States of America

QuadGraphics, 2020

ISBN: 978-1-7341330-0-4 (Hardcover)
ISBN: 978-1-7341330-1-1 (E-Book)

Experimental Aircraft Association, Inc.
3000 Poberezny Road
Oshkosh, WI 54902

Publisher: Jack J. Pelton
Editor in Chief: James Busha
Senior Editor: Hal Bryan
Senior Copy Editor: Colleen Walsh
Assistant Editor: Ti Windisch
Copy Editor: Jen Knaack
Production Coordinator: Kayla Floyd
Graphic Design Manager: Brandon Jacobs
Digital Marketing Manager: Sara Nisler

THE FINAL MISSION

**PERSONAL STORIES OF THE LIVES TOUCHED
BY EAA'S B-17, *ALUMINUM OVERCAST***

BY CHRIS HENRY

WITH HAL BRYAN

FOREWORD BY COL. FRANK BORMAN AND DR. HARRY FRIEDMAN

THIS BOOK IS RESPECTFULLY DEDICATED TO THE VETERANS
WHO MANNED THE MIGHTY FLYING FORTRESS,
THOSE BRAVE YOUNG MEN WHO RISKED — AND OFTEN LOST —
IT ALL IN HUMANITY'S SINGLE GREATEST FIGHT AGAINST TYRANNY.

THEY WERE JUST KIDS BACK THEN, BUT THEY LOOM LIKE GIANTS
IN HISTORY AS WE STAND HUMBLY ON THEIR SHOULDERS.

WE OWE THEM A DEBT THAT CAN NEVER BE REPAID,
AND MUST NEVER BE FORGOTTEN.

EXCLUSIVE CONTENT

Throughout this book, you will see QR codes like the one to the right. Simply open the camera app on your smartphone or tablet, point it at the code, and follow the link onscreen. You will automatically be directed to exclusive videos that take you deeper into the lives of B-17 veterans, and enable you to experience our Flying Fortress, *Aluminum Overcast*, firsthand.

EXPERIENCE
ALUMINUM
Overcast

FOREWORD

AMERICANS ARE FAR MORE LIKELY to focus on the future than reflect on the past. This attitude is important in a democratic society because the motivation there is always to improve. It is, however, necessary to also understand how we got to the present. To do that we must examine the events of the past that made us who we are today.

Of all the great events in American history none required a greater national effort than World War II. It is hard for us to understand the scope of that effort. Americans experienced rationing, the first peacetime draft, and many military casualties. The home front mobilized to make weapons of war. America produced about two-thirds of all of the materiel used by the Allied nations to defeat the Axis powers.

In this classic battle of good versus evil, the U.S. armed forces started growing from 227,000 personnel in 1939 to 12,000,000 by 1945. President Roosevelt placed increasing emphasis on upgrading the striking power of the Army Air Corps. By the time Pearl Harbor was attacked in 1941, Congress had spent more for Army procurement than it had for both the Army and Navy during all of World War I. In January 1942 the president called for 60,000 aircraft to be built in 1942 and 125,000 more in 1943. To support this effort the federal budget increased from $8.9 billion in 1939 to $95 billion in 1945. More than 270,000 aircraft of all types (almost 13,000 of which were B-17s) were produced in this country during the war, and a staggering 57,000 were lost.

One of America's core strategic policies was daylight precision bombing of enemy industries. The 8th Air Force based in England led the effort in Europe. The groups flying the B-17 were the heart of the 8th Air Force. Those B-17 groups of the 8th flew more missions, dropped more bombs, and suffered more casualties than any other force involved in the European air war.

Chris Henry has produced a wonderful book that honors the memory of the men who manned the B-17s. Using interviews with survivors plus new and old photographs, Chris helps us understand the enormous debt every free human owes the men who crewed the B-17s.

—
FRANK BORMAN, EAA Lifetime 300174, was the commander of the Apollo 8 mission to the moon, was the CEO of Eastern Air Lines, and recently donated a substantial collection of artifacts to the EAA Aviation Museum.

BY COL. FRANK BORMAN

BY DR. HARRY FRIEDMAN

IN MILITARY LITERATURE we read of battles, raids, and fighting machines. Two groups are involved in these actions. There are the men and women who carried the war to the enemy. Then there are the descendants who honor those warriors. In these pages, we have the opportunity to hear from the veterans who performed in extreme conditions and were able to come back to tell us their stories. Thankfully, we have these few stories because so much of that history went to the graves of those who could not talk about their experiences. In these stories, we learn of the professionalism of the aviators and ground crews, the humor that they were able to find, and also the tragedies of the wounded and dying. Chris Henry and his co-workers have done a great service to the veterans, their families, and the reader. They started out intending to honor our veterans by inviting them and their families to fly on EAA's B-17, named *Aluminum Overcast*. They quickly learned there were tales being told by these oftentimes reluctant veterans. Chris has a remarkable ability to draw out the memories that these veterans were internalizing. He quickly recognized that he was in a unique position to preserve and share the memories of these veterans for history, and fortunately for us he has written this book.

I can appreciate firsthand what his challenge was. When the *Memphis Belle* was on display in Memphis, many veterans of the air war in Europe visited. Some became docents telling their stories. It was not uncommon for three generations of a family to visit together. To watch the emotions on the faces of these former airmen as they gazed at the *Memphis Belle* was a heartwarming experience for us. It enabled them to open up about their past. There were those who would start talking about being on an airplane like the *Memphis Belle*, sometimes seeming to be talking to no one in particular or occasionally to a grandchild. Imagine the surprise expressed by the son or daughter upon hearing these stories for the first time. Just being in the presence of such a machine allows the veterans to open up.

This is what Chris Henry has done. As if collecting stories from the veterans was not enough, he surpassed himself by arranging a 10-man crew of veterans to be assembled and fly off into the cold sky in *Aluminum Overcast* as they did many years before. What an achievement this was and no doubt presented a moment of supreme satisfaction to Chris, EAA, and the fortunate veterans who took that flight.

Please enjoy this book. I needn't remind you that by the time you read it, some of the vets will have died. But for Chris Henry's interviews, you would not be able to hear these fellows tell it like it was.

—
DR. HARRY FRIEDMAN, EAA 164173, Warbirds 3597, is a Memphis Belle Memorial Association board member, and co-author of the book *Memphis Belle: Dispelling the Myths.*

INTRODUCTION

AS I WRITE THIS, I am sitting in EAA's Kermit Weeks Hangar in Oshkosh, Wisconsin, near the rear entry hatch of a B-17 Flying Fortress. I'm looking at the airplane and thinking about the amazing men who pulled themselves through that hatch mission after mission. They knew the odds were stacked against them, yet they went anyway. I think about the people whose lives are embodied in this one airplane. The engineers who first designed it, the workers who built it, the pilots and crew members who fought on board it. And of course, the ones who died on it. I never imagined that I would get to be a part of such an amazing airplane. We have witnessed incredible moments on this airframe. The heroes who have crawled through those doorways, and the stories that have been told on board. I cannot help but feel proud of what our team has accomplished and continues to do.

I grew up in Pittsburgh, Pennsylvania. My father was a steelworker, and my mother works in a school. My childhood home was on the approach to Pittsburgh International Airport. As a young kid I would go outside and watch the jets line up for the approach. Then one day my uncle brought me an airplane magazine featuring World War II aircraft. After that everything I did involved airplanes. It was not long before that love of airplanes started showing up in books, models, and a need to go to the local air show every year. When I was at the air show, I was introduced to the B-17 in person. The first one I saw was *Texas Raiders*. I can still remember climbing up the ladder into the front crew hatch with my grandfather. After that, he showed me a movie called *Twelve O'Clock High*. A few years later the B-17 *Nine-O-Nine* — since destroyed in a tragic crash — had a landing accident at the air show, and for the next several years it was under restoration at the nearby Air Heritage Museum. I was just 12 years old, but the volunteers at the museum said they could use the help. My mother and father decided to let me volunteer to see if it would become more than just a passing interest. As it turned out, it became a lifestyle. My mom would usually drive me to the museum on Saturday mornings to volunteer for the day, but sometimes my father would drive, even after working a 12-hour night shift in the steel mill, and we would stop for an early breakfast on the way to the airfield. I can never thank them enough for what they gave me. My parents worked closely with the museum volunteers to make sure I was looked after. Thanks to

longtime aviation professionals Clair Pazey, Bob Huddock, Bob and Rob Morelli, and many others, a young kid who knew nothing got a great foundation in aviation history. I would not get to do the things I do today if it weren't for them taking a chance on a kid and providing that pathway into aviation. I had the privilege to learn about missions and life in WWII directly from the men and women who fought in it. We had pilots, crew members, and mechanics all working to restore these old aircraft to their former glory. I am lucky to have had the chance to work in that hangar and soak it all up, and I've been involved in aviation ever since. I also have a promise to fulfill to my friend Clair. I once thanked him for everything he had done for me.

"If you get the chance to help someone else get going in airplanes, help them," he said. "That is how you can thank me." We live in a fast-paced world. It is easy to see this airplane out somewhere, check it out for a minute, and then get on with your day. For many, WWII is quickly becoming ancient history. Some of the younger generations feel so removed from it that they compare it to the Civil War. For many, it is just an old airplane. But it is more. When we can get to a place where we talk not only about technical data like airspeeds and horsepower, but also about the lives that this aircraft touched and continues to touch, that's when the real lessons are learned. When you hear the human side of the missions that aircraft like this flew, that is where history comes alive.

This is the mission that EAA fulfills with the B-17 next to me. Like so many before it, it has a name — *Aluminum Overcast*. The name is proudly painted on the nose of the aircraft along with a pretty blonde pinup girl in a red bathing suit. When I first started working at EAA, I hoped to have some stories to tell involving this aircraft, but never could I have predicted the journey that lay ahead. The pages that follow are filled with some of the milestones of that journey. The stories have been recorded just as they were told to me from the veterans and their families. Some of them are about the good times; many of them are about the rough times. Something that we must always remember is that a spot on a B-17 was considered one of the more dangerous places to serve during the war. By the time WWII ended, the 8th Air Force, one of the primary operators of the B-17, would lose more men than the entire Marine Corps. I felt that I owed it to the men and women of the greatest generation to tell their stories just as they told them to me. History has no respect for political correctness — war, even less so. Many of the airplanes featured in this book have names and artwork on them that are risqué. That should come as no surprise when you consider that these airplanes were operated — and, thus, decorated — by kids in their late teens and early 20s. The average age of a B-17 pilot was just 21 years old, while the average age of a gunner was closer to 18. Many of the crew members came from small towns, and in many cases, the first time they ever flew on an aircraft was in the military. They found themselves in foreign countries thousands of miles from home, shivering in frigid battlefields more than 5 miles high. Thanks to the best efforts and grim determination of an enemy that was disciplined, well trained, and technologically advanced, the odds of coming home were not in their favor. When you put the fate of the free world on the shoulders of kids, it's easy to forgive a pinup painted on the nose of an airplane, boosting morale and giving the crews an identity.

While you read this book, I hope you reflect on the fact that these were real people who flew these dangerous missions. The next time you're on the street, at the bank, or at the grocery store and see an older gentleman wearing a WWII veteran hat, take a moment to talk to him and, especially, to say thank you. Remember what he did several decades ago to earn that hat and, in so doing, to grant you the freedom and way of life you enjoy today.

▲ A photo of me (at right), Rob Morelli, and another volunteer as we work on the the B-17 that portrayed the *Memphis Belle* in the 1990 film.

"WHY, IT'S A FLYING FORTRESS"

I n the mid-1930s the United States was in the middle of the Great Depression. Even the armed forces weren't immune from the ravaging effects on the economy, as the U.S. Army and the Navy were at odds and regularly competed for more funding. The U.S. Army Air Corps (USAAC) made an announcement on August 8, 1934, that it was looking to develop a new aircraft — a bomber capable of reinforcing the air forces in Hawaii, Panama, and Alaska. The requirements specified that it must carry a "useful bomb load" at an altitude of 10,000 feet for 10 hours with a top speed of at least 200 mph, and all this with a required range of 2,000 miles. Several manufacturers bid on the project, building prototypes at their own expense. While some companies chose to simply modify an already existing airframe, Boeing went for a completely different approach.

◀ The B-17E prototype flying over Seattle in September 1941.

It staked the future of the company on the project designated Model 299. Boeing assigned designers E. Gifford Emery and Edward Curtis Wells the task of creating the machine, and it was built out of Boeing's own budget. Little did Emery and Wells know they were about to create a legend in aviation history.

The new aircraft was influenced by some of Boeing's earlier designs such as the B-15 bomber and Model 247 airliner. It had a wingspan of 103 feet and 9 inches, a dimension that remained unchanged throughout the entire run of B-17 production, and was just shy of 75 feet long. It was the first Boeing military design to feature an enclosed flight deck rather than an open cockpit. Four engines powered it, but Boeing boasted that it could fly easily on three. The aircraft was equipped with five .30-caliber machine guns, and it was capable of hauling 4,800 pounds of bombs at a range of more than 2,000 miles. The entire process from design to flight test was less than a year.

▲ In honor of the 75th anniversary of Hill Air Force Base, our *Aluminum Overcast* flew over Hangar One. The base is named for Maj. Ployer "Pete" Hill, who died while testing the Boeing Model 299.

▲ The Boeing Model 299 after the crash on October 30, 1935, which destroyed Boeing's only prototype and took them out of the running for the Army's multiengine bomber contract.

On July 1, 1935, rollout day arrived. It was time to unveil the new design to the public and the media. The last 11 months of hard work was about to see the light of day. During the build the workers had been sworn to secrecy as Boeing had a fear of industrial espionage. As the aircraft cleared the hangar doors, bristling with its multiple machine guns, *Seattle Times* reporter Richard Williams remarked, "Why, it's a flying fortress!" Boeing quickly adopted and trademarked the name. On July 28, the day of its fateful first flight, Boeing chief test pilot Leslie "Les" Tower took the controls. The aircraft performed flawlessly, and it was time to get to Wright Field in Dayton, Ohio, for the competition that would determine which company's design would be awarded the contract. On August 20 the Model 299 departed for Dayton and completed the 2,000-mile trip in a record-breaking nine hours, faster than the pursuit aircraft of the day. The other main competitors in the flyoff were the Douglas DB-1 and the Martin Model 146. The DB-1 would later become the B-18. This aircraft was in large part a modified Douglas DC-2 airliner. The Martin 146 was in many ways a scaled-up version of the company's aging B-10.

It was not long before the Boeing 299's competitive performance and long range placed it far ahead of the other entries. During the course of the competition, the Model 299 was redesignated the B-17. Before the competition was complete, the USAAC discussed purchasing 65 of the new Boeing bombers; however, Boeing's luck changed on October 30, 1935. Army Air Corps test pilot Maj. Ployer Peter "Pete" Hill and Boeing test pilot Les Tower were assigned to take the Model 299 on an acceptance flight. They forgot to disengage the control locks, which locked control surfaces in place while the aircraft was parked. As the aircraft neared takeoff speed it entered a steep climb, stalled, nosed over, and crashed. Both pilots died in the crash. Many questioned whether the 299 was too complex of a machine for people to operate. The promised order of 65 aircraft was canceled, and the USAAC ordered 220 of the less expensive Douglas B-18 Bolos. While examining the events that led to the 299 crash, it was decided that a list of items should be checked prior to operating any aircraft. This eventually took the form of the modern checklist still in use today by pilots around the world. Eighty years later, we took Pete Hill's daughter flying with us in our B-17. The aircraft her father gave his life proving has become a legend.

▲ Early B-17s being rolled out of Plant 2. Mainly made by hand, the early models, sometimes called "shark-finned" variants, are arguably among the most beautiful aircraft built. Don England saved this rare photo as the plant was being torn down in 2010. He found it in a trash can and, luckily for us, saved it from being lost forever.

Regardless of the crash, many high-ranking officials in the Army Air Corps were still impressed by the performance of the 299. Through a legal loophole, which allowed the USAAC to spend money on special test vehicles, they were able to purchase 13 examples of the Boeing design. These first examples were designated YB-17s to denote where the funding came from to purchase them. They took 11 months to build and were largely handmade. The first YB-17s were assigned to the 2nd Bombardment Group based at Langley Field in Virginia for operational development and flight tests. The Army Air Corps wasted no time in showing off its new bombers. It was part of Gen. Frank Maxwell Andrews' plan to gain public support for the Army Air Corps. On May 12, 1938, on one of their first missions, three B-17s, directed by lead navigator Lt. Curtis LeMay, were sent by Andrews to "intercept" and photograph the Italian ocean liner Rex. The Rex was 610 miles off the Atlantic coast.

▲ Another Don England photo, which we are fortunate he saved. At the time this photo was taken in Seattle, this was most of the existing B-17 fleet.

The mission was successful and widely publicized. It also infuriated Navy officials, who saw the Navy as the defender of the coast, and they approached Congress to try to restrict B-17 flights to over the continental United States. The B-17 was destined to change history and be a part of it.

The first B-17s to see combat were not in the USAAC. Under the Lend-Lease Act, B-17C and B-17D models were given to the Royal Air Force, which called the airplane the Fortress I. The RAF evaluated the aircraft and said it was a good performer but lacked in a few areas, including rear firepower and armor. Boeing went back to the drawing board and developed the new B-17E model. This aircraft featured powered gun turrets as well as a rear tail gunner compartment known as the "stinger" tail. The waist gun blisters were gone, and windows took their place. The first B-17Es were assigned to what by then had become the U.S. Army Air Forces' 19th Bomb Group. These brand new B-17s were deployed to Clark Field in the Philippines just weeks before the attack on Pearl Harbor. As anyone who has studied history or seen the movie *Tora! Tora! Tora!* knows, B-17s were en route to Pearl

Harbor the morning of the attacks on December 7, 1941. An American radar outpost even mistook some of the attacking Japanese aircraft for the flight of Flying Fortresses. These B-17s arrived low on fuel, with no ammunition, and under attack. The guns onboard were still packed away in shipping crates. Not a great way to fly into the middle of a war.

America had entered World War II, and now it was going to need as many B-17s as it could get. Factories modernized — gone were the days of building aircraft by hand. Large assembly lines now pumped out B-17s at a staggering rate. At the height of production, three companies were producing 130 B-17s a week. The Boeing plant in Seattle alone was producing 16 per day. Women came to work on the assembly lines to replace the men who were now in combat.

While we usually think of the B-17 fighting in Europe, the type did plenty in the Pacific theater as well. The B-17 saw action at the Battle of Midway, Rabaul, and countless other locations. They hunted out targets and fought back against Japanese fighters. The crews fought with the feeling that each bomb dropped, each fighter destroyed, was in some small way a payback for Pearl Harbor. The B-17 held the line until Consolidated B-24 bombers started to show up in force and make up the backbone of the Pacific operations.

The B-17s would become famous for their missions in the European theater, however. Their daring daylight raids at times used 1,000 planes. English civilians nicknamed these mass formations "Aluminum Overcast."

The B-17 was able to carry 8,000 pounds of bombs on a mission at an altitude of 35,000 feet at a range of more than 2,000 miles. While flying at altitude the temperature could hit as low as 60 degrees below zero. For this reason crew members were equipped with heated electric flight suits that plugged into the airplane's power system, heavy gloves, goggles, a winter hat, and an oxygen mask. They also had to wear an uncomfortable throat microphone so they could communicate with one another. Onboard the B-17 a unique bond formed. This 10-man crew was a team working to keep one another alive, taking it just one mission at a time.

While en route to a target each member of the crew had a specific role to ensure that the mission was successful and the crew came back alive. The gunners were in charge of defending the heavy bomb-laden aircraft from enemy fighters. Gunners were aided in this by the pilots who flew in a box formation, an idea that was originated by LeMay, the navigator from the early testing days of the B-17 who would eventually retire as a four-star general. This gave the gunners their best amount of coverage and some help to ensure they were not firing into friendly aircraft. Using this formation the B-17s could aim as many as 500 machine guns at a target, providing a blanket of cover. It took a lot of effort and concentration on the part of the pilots to fly the tight formations, but the benefits were many. Once they started flying the new formation, the enemy fighters started feeling the toll. Navigators ensured the aircraft found their targets and avoided those areas with heavy flak coverage. The bombardier cared for his bomb load as well as the bombsight. Once the bombing run began, it was the bombardier's show to run. After all, the whole point of the mission was to drop bombs on the target.

As the war continued, the bombers flew deeper into Germany, a risky proposition with the German Luftwaffe on the prowl. The toll on the bomber crews added up quickly, especially those missions that required crews to fly over Germany for several hours with no fighter escort. While many bombers never returned, the crew members of those that did owed their lives to the rugged design of the B-17 and its ability to return home with massive combat damage. Some aircraft found a way to limp home and brought their crews home safely, but the damage was so extensive that they never flew again. Sometimes entire squadrons were shredded with only a few planes returning from a mission. This eventually forced a change in tactics in the U.S. bombing campaign.

The largest change in tactics was the addition of escort fighters to protect the bombers, and then allowing these fighters to destroy the German air force at will. These aircraft became known as "little friends." The main aircraft used were the Lockheed P-38 Lightning, Republic P-47 Thunderbolt, and the North American P-51 Mustang. These aircraft, fitted with external fuel tanks or drop tanks, were able to help the bombers fight their way to the target.

Before the war's end, just shy of 13,000 B-17s were built. This required around-the-clock work from not just Boeing, but also Lockheed subsidiary Vega and Douglas Aircraft. Today, fewer than 50 airframes exist. They are treasures used to honor, remember, and educate. To those who flew on them and built them they take on another meaning. Their time serving with the aircraft may have been relatively short, but it was also defining.

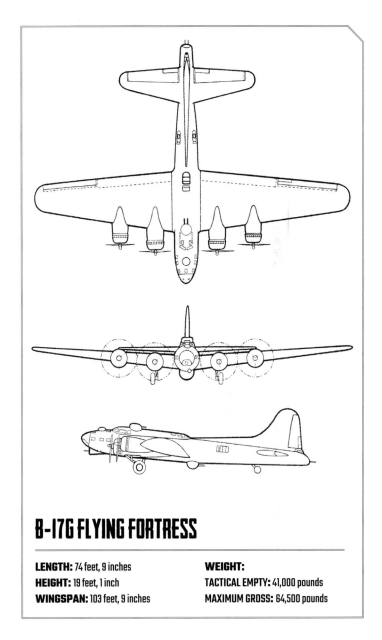

B-17G FLYING FORTRESS

LENGTH: 74 feet, 9 inches
HEIGHT: 19 feet, 1 inch
WINGSPAN: 103 feet, 9 inches

WEIGHT:
TACTICAL EMPTY: 41,000 pounds
MAXIMUM GROSS: 64,500 pounds

For many surviving crew members, the way they want history to remember them is as those who served their country aboard the mighty Flying Fortress.

N5017N

May 18, 1945, was just another day at the Lockheed-Vega B-17 production plant. In support of the war effort, companies were allowed to manufacture another company's product to ensure that the United States had enough. A great example of this was B-17 production. Even though the B-17 was a Boeing aircraft, more were needed than Boeing could produce. Douglas Aircraft in Long Beach as well as Lockheed Vega in Burbank, California, also produced the B-17. On this May day, B-17G-105-VE, serial No. 44-85740, rolled down the assembly line and was accepted into the U.S. Army Air Forces' inventory. By the time this B-17 was ready for combat, however, the operations were coming to a close. The aircraft was sent to storage in New York and then eventually to Altus, Oklahoma, on November 7, 1945.

While in Altus, the aircraft was sold for scrap for $750. An aerial mapping company named Universal Aviation purchased -740 and registered it as N5017N. On August 2, 1947, the aircraft was sold to Charles T. Winters, of Miami, Florida, who in turn sold it on August 16, 1947, to Joe Lopez of the Vero Beach Import and Export Co., who purchased the aircraft to haul cattle between Florida and Puerto Rico. Its new role necessitated removing the original radio compartment and floor, replacing it with a strengthened floor. In 1949, Aero Service Corp. bought the aircraft and turned it into an aerial photography and surveying platform. For the next 12 years N5017N carried out mapping operations over Saudi Arabia, Libya, Lebanon, Iran, Laos, Vietnam, Cambodia, Egypt, and Jordan.

In 1962 Chris D. Stoltzfus and Associates purchased the aircraft to use as a fire ant sprayer. The conversion didn't happen and the airplane was sold in 1966 to Dothan Aviation Corp., where it was finally fitted with spray bars and a chemical hopper. It worked as a sprayer for the next 10 years. From 1976 on, the aircraft was parked in outdoor storage. Now long obsolete, this B-17 was nearing its end until Dr. Bill Harrison bought it in 1978. Owning warbirds was nothing new for Bill. He had owned several aircraft, including Mustangs and Sea Furys, since the 1960s. The B-17, however, was the king of the warbirds. A glamorous aircraft to restore and operate.

▲ Currently the oldest known photo of our B-17. This is N5017N, the aircraft that would become *Aluminum Overcast*. Taken just after the war in the late 1940s, this photo comes from the Stoltzfus family, who bought our future airplane in 1962 for $10,000.

"A friend of mine said that he had seen a few B-17s just parked and sitting in Dothan, Alabama," Bill said in an interview. "He had heard that they were full of corrosion. My friend Tony was going to be in the area and said that he would check them out for me." What Tony found was anything but corroded aircraft. The aircraft had been converted by taking out the bulkheads between the radio room and bomb bay, making one large, sealed unit to carry a chemical called Mirex that was used to combat fire ants. Spray booms ran out 120 feet down the wings and extended beyond the tips. While many spray aircraft suffer corrosion issues from the chemicals being used, the Mirex in N5017N was mixed with soybean oil and cornmeal, so it was noncorrosive. In fact, it actually sealed the aircraft from corrosion.

"We would have to sweep up corn after shutting down the aircraft for years." Bill said. The B-17s were in overall great shape.

Bill purchased the aircraft for the "B-17s Around the World" program.

"I had the choice of buying both aircraft and all of the parts or one aircraft and half of the parts. I went with the latter," Bill said. It first went to Griffin, Georgia, where the spray booms and hopper were removed. On the way to its first air show appearance Bill was flying the aircraft in formation with a group of friends who followed in escort fighters.

"We were on our way to the 1979 Miami air races. I was in the B-17, and I was in formation with a few P-51s. I could not see one of the Mustangs. I called out for George Roberts, the man flying the one I could not see. He replied that he was below me flying in my shadow, and that it was like being in an *Aluminum Overcast*." That story combined with the name that the British civilians gave the large bomber formations is how our B-17 *Aluminum Overcast* got its name. Soon thereafter, the group donated the aircraft to the Experimental Aircraft Association.

Aluminum Overcast was put on display in what is now the EAA Aviation Museum in Oshkosh, Wisconsin, for the next few years while a major restoration began. This effort was to take the airplane and return it as closely as EAA could to a combat configuration. Due to the extensive modifications made when converting it to a spray aircraft, a total reconfiguration of the navigator, waist, radio room, and other compartments was needed. Top and ball turrets were located, and original military equipment such as radio gear and a Norden bombsight were sourced and installed. The aircraft was painted in the colors of the 398th Bomb Group, 601st Bomb Squadron — and the painting was completed with the help of combat veterans from the 398th Bomb Group.

The aircraft set out in 1994 on its first tour. Since then *Aluminum Overcast* has been flying around the country, touching lives wherever it lands. It serves in many roles today, but one of the most powerful roles is that of healer. It has brought peace to many of our veterans and family members who came to see it. Many of the veterans had stories that they had kept inside for decades. Then the sights and smell of this aircraft brought them back, and they were able to share with our crews and families about their experiences. Many times the stories were being told for the first time.

It's strange, perhaps, that an aircraft built for war now brings peace to older generations and a flying history lesson to younger ones. Our aircraft has been on a great adventure — one that keeps going. This book collects just a few of the stories of those who flew with us onboard our B-17, stories that have waited too long for the telling. These are the stories of the boys of the Flying Fortress.

▲ N5017N flying over the terminal building at Wheelless Airport near Dothan, Alabama, in 1968.

▲ In this 1974 photo, N5017N is rigged with equipment used to fight fire ants.

▲ The first version of the name and artwork that would come to define our B-17. Bill Harrison had the artwork applied after a trip to the 1979 Miami air races.

"THIS IS NO DRILL"

BY DECEMBER 1941 the B-17 had evolved up through the E model. While production was steady, Boeing wasn't cranking them out in large numbers because, unlike our Allies in Europe, the United States wasn't directly involved in the developing world war. But that was about to change.

◄ American sailors at Ford Island Naval Air Station reacting to the explosion of the USS Shaw during the second wave of attacks on the U.S. naval base at Pearl Harbor, December 7, 1941.

EARL COOPER

WHEN WISCONSIN NATIVE Earl Cooper's nephew came to visit our aircraft over its winter maintenance, he had a powerful story to tell. His Uncle Earl was on the infamous flight of B-17s coming over from the mainland to Pearl Harbor on December 7. As they neared the field they saw some small aircraft that they believed were Navy aircraft attempting to show off for their arrival. As they started their descent, though, the crew could just make out the Japanese insignia on what had just become enemy fighters. Earl's nephew told us that his uncle's crew passed over battleship row and could see the devastation, including the destroyed battleship USS Arizona.

HENNING ELSASSER

HENNING ELSASSER was a B-17 gunner in the 5th Bomb Group at Hickam Field in Hawaii. On the quiet morning of December 7, 1941, he was asleep in his bunk. His friend awakened him with the news that the Japanese were attacking, yelling about the enemy airplanes overhead. They ran outside just as the Japanese airplanes strafed their barracks. News traveled much slower then, and Henning could not quickly get word out to his folks and fiancée in a small town just outside of Omaha, Nebraska, that he had survived the attacks.

"We will not buy a Christmas tree until I know if my son is alive," his mother said at the time. "If he has been killed, we will not be celebrating Christmas."

In a town as small as theirs where everyone knew one another, news traveled fast. Everyone in the community hoped and prayed for word of Henning's survival.

Finally, the good news came in the form of a telegram. It didn't say much, but it said enough — Henning was alive and well. This was the best present his mother could have asked for, and the family went straight into town and bought a Christmas tree. As they drove home, their friends and neighbors lined the streets, cheering and applauding.

Henning went on to crew a B-17 at Guadalcanal, through the Southwest Pacific, and in the Battle of Midway, where even after being wounded his crew managed to shoot down two enemy aircraft and track a Japanese task force. He returned home to a hero's welcome and married his fiancée in a ceremony that was standing room only. Members of the Elsasser family flew on EAA's B-17 on November 22, 2015, in Topeka, Kansas.

EUGENE "DUTCH" BENEDETTI

MAJ. DUTCH BENEDETTI, who served with the 19th Bomb Group, 65th Bomb Squadron, was born in Roseville, California, on February 10, 1915. He flew B-17s in the Pacific theater. His crew trained in their downtime so that each member had a few chances to fly the airplane in case they ever needed to take over. On a raid on Rabaul, while flying a B-17E named *Old Faithful*, Japanese Zero aircraft attacked them. Shells came through the cockpit, and Dutch was hit in the back of the head. Despite being in great pain, he continued to fly the airplane until the top turret gunner noticed. Even after being injected with morphine, he stayed at the controls and helped belly land the airplane back at base. It took 70 years for Dutch's actions to be recognized, but he was eventually awarded the Silver Star Medal. When his daughter, Janis, flew with us, she was wearing her father's flight jacket and medals.

▲ The B-17 flown by Capt. Raymond T. Swenson of the 38th Reconnaissance Squadron. The airplane was strafed by a Japanese Zero after landing, igniting the flares onboard.

▶ The same B-17 pictured in a famous photo taken later, after the engines had been salvaged.

▼ After attacking Capt. Swenson's B-17, Zero AI-154 turned toward Hickam Field. Gunners from the USS Helm (DD-388) fired at it, and the enemy fighter crashed into a building. The wreckage was moved into a hangar at Hickam as the USAAC began to study it.

HEWITT T. "SHORTY" WHELESS

LT. HEWITT T. "SHORTY" WHELESS was more than likely one of the first combat pilots flying the B-17. Assigned to the 19th Bomb Group, he was flying patrol missions in a B-17D just a week after the attack on Pearl Harbor. During one of these daring early missions, his aircraft was attacked by a formation of Japanese aircraft. The B-17 took multiple hits, but at the end of the fight it was still flying. Shorty and his crew claimed seven enemy aircraft destroyed. Once they returned to base, the aircraft landed on three flat tires. This contact with the enemy was such a boost to American morale that President Roosevelt mentioned the incident in his April 28, 1942, fireside chat. Crew member Michael Digangi found out that Lt. Wheless's daughter was flying with us and made sure to bring it to our attention.

▶ After Lt. Wheless and his crew fought off Japanese attacks and brought their battle-damaged B-17 home, they were sent off to make appearances, like this one in front of a factory-fresh B-17E, to foster support for the war effort.

TRAINING FOR WAR

Pearl Harbor is forever synonymous with our entry into World War II. The events of December 7, 1941, were so powerful, so life changing, that years later, anyone who was alive can still remember where they were and what they were doing when they heard of the attack. Much like younger generations remember the John F. Kennedy assassination, the moon landing, and 9/11, everyone has a different story about Pearl Harbor. Some were working at a job when they heard the news, while others were in school when they found out about the attack. Many had no idea where Pearl Harbor was. The one thing that holds true for almost everyone was the feeling that it was time to go to war. On December 8, President Roosevelt proclaimed that December 7 would be "a date which will live in infamy." He also promised the American people that we would see our way through to absolute victory. In the days that followed the attacks on Pearl Harbor by the Japanese, Germany announced its alliance with Japan and declared war on the United States. The United States, after years of working to stay out of the war, was now fully involved.

America was behind the power curve militarily in those early days of the war. To win this war we would have to come together and come from behind. This would mean years of war bond drives, rationing of everyday items for the war efforts, victory gardens, scrap drives, and blackouts. However, when this sleeping giant awoke, it did so with a vengeance. Armed forces recruiting centers had lines out of the doors and down the streets in many towns. One veteran told me, "If you didn't sign up for the service after Pearl Harbor, many felt that there was something wrong with you or that you were a coward. One guy in our town found out he was classified as 4-F, which meant 'not acceptable for service in the armed forces.' He went home and killed himself."

As a bomber crew member during World War II, the primary factor in your assignment came down to rank — officer or enlisted. Pilots, bombardiers, and navigators were all officer positions. Then there were the enlisted positions of gunner, flight engineer, and radio operator. Each position went through its specific training before being assigned to a crew. Pilots learned to fly at training bases throughout the country. They learned in basic, primary, advanced, and then multiengine aircraft. Future bomber pilots started in aircraft like the Boeing PT-17 Stearman or Ryan PT-22 Recruit, then trained in the North American AT-6 Texan, and transitioned to multiengine trainers like the Beechcraft AT-10, Cessna AT-17, or Curtiss AT-9 Jeep before training in the B-17. New pilots trained with instructors who walked them through the finer points of flying the big bomber.

▲ Future B-17 pilot Ed Stevens is seen here as a cadet in front of a PT-17 Stearman he trained in.

Bombardiers went through a special school and learned how to operate the new Norden bombsight. One of these schools was located in Midland, Texas. Bombardiers also swore an oath to protect the bombsight from ever falling into the hands of the enemy. The oath was, "Mindful of the secret trust about to be placed in me by my Commander in Chief, the President of the United States, by whose direction I have been chosen for bombardier training, and mindful of the fact that I am to become guardian of one of my country's most priceless military assets, the American bombsight, I do here, in the presence of Almighty God, swear by the Bombardier's Code of Honor to keep inviolate the secrecy of any and all confidential information revealed to me, and further to uphold the honor and integrity of the Army Air Forces, if need be, with my life itself." This was an oath that was not to be taken lightly.

Navigators attended advanced training schools where they studied skills such as chart reading, deduced or dead reckoning, and celestial navigation, using tools of the trade like the sextant. They pored over charts with plotters and circular slide rules, things that may seem quaint and dated but are actually still familiar to modern pilots.

The gunners onboard a Flying Fortress were in charge of defending the bomber from enemy fighter attacks. To do that, they had to know their machine gun inside and out. They needed to be able to dismantle their weapon and put it back together in record time, under miserable conditions. They learned the basics of marksmanship, including how to lead a moving target, as well as things like ammunition conservation by disciplining themselves to fire only in short bursts. They spent time studying enemy fighter pilot tactics, as well.

The homefront in America would become a force to be reckoned with. Manufacturers of traditional consumer items such as cars and home furnishings were now building bombers and tanks. The Ford Motor Co. built the jeep along with Bantam and Willys. Ford also built the B-24 Liberator in its Ypsilanti, Michigan, plant. Cities like Pittsburgh, Pennsylvania; Toledo, Ohio; and Burbank, California, became industrial giants. Before the war was over, Lockheed Vega built 2,750 B-17s in its Burbank plant, while Douglas would complete 3,000 of the bombers in its Santa Monica factory. Boeing itself would produce 6,981 of what was destined to become one of its most historic aircraft.

▲ A young Lt. Howard Krasemann taxies out in his BT-13 Valiant, better known by its nickname, the "Vultee Vibrator."

▲ Lt. Bob Abresch pictured during basic flight training in a BT-13 at Goodfellow Field, near San Angelo, Texas. He would go on to fly 33 missions in B-17s in the 398th Bomb Group.

THE BLOODY YANKS ARRIVE IN EUROPE

In the dark early years of the war in Europe, the Royal Air Force held its ground against the German Luftwaffe. While RAF Bomber Command attempted daylight bombing early on, it found greater success — and, more importantly, lower attrition — flying night missions. In May 1942 the wheels of an American B-17 bomber touched down on the soil of England for the first time. A new bomber force was being organized, and at the spearhead of all of this was to be the 8th Air Force. History remembers them as the "Mighty Eighth." The main difference between RAF and USAAF operations was that the U.S. Army Air Forces was going to focus on daylight bombing of strategic targets. Based on their own disastrous attempts, RAF personnel were opposed to daylight bombing and tried to convince the USAAF not to attempt it. Sir Arthur "Bomber" Harris, the head of RAF Bomber Command, appealed to Prime Minister Winston Churchill to convince President Roosevelt not to attempt it. FDR said he had faith in his combat commanders and would continue with what they ordered. None of this was known to the combat crews flying the daring daylight missions at the time.

The biggest card in the USAAF's hand was the Norden bombsight. The Norden used an analog computer and an autopilot that enabled bombardiers to hit their targets with unprecedented precision. While flying between bases in the United States, the bombsights were taken out of the aircraft and placed in guarded vaults. If the bombardier had to bail out of a stricken aircraft, he was to destroy the bombsight so that it would not fall into the hands of the enemy. The first USAAF bombing mission in Europe would take place on August 17, 1942. The lead aircraft, a B-17 named *Butcher Shop*, was piloted by Maj. Paul Tibbets, best known in history as the pilot of the B-29 *Enola Gay*. Gen. Ira Eaker, who had helped organize the YB-17s intercepting the Rex to demonstrate the validity of air power, and was now in command of the 8th Air Force, observed the raid from aboard another B-17, *Yankee Doodle*. The raid on the railroad marshalling yards at Sotteville-lès-Rouen in France was flown by 12 B-17Es of the 97th Bomb Group. It was around this time that the first B-17Fs were brought to England. The F model and later G model made up the bulk of the B-17s that fought over Europe.

▲ Charles Ormsby and his 398th Bomb Group crew on leave at Piccadilly Circus in London.

Each aircraft was initially crewed by 10 men, though that number would be reduced later in the war. They were young men of all backgrounds, most of them aged 18-22, and they came from big cities as well as small rural towns all across America. The British said that the Americans were "overpaid, oversexed, and over here." One look at a few of the noses of our aircraft may explain that thought. Many of the crews painted artwork on the noses of their airplanes along with a name. Many times it was cartoon characters, nicknames, funny jokes among the crews, but their favorite subject was girls. Paintings inspired by popular pinup artists like Alberto Vargas and George Petty adorned many of the B-17s in combat. Col. Robert Morgan, the pilot of the famous *Memphis Belle*, once said he was sure that the German pilots must have thought that a lingerie catalog was coming at them since the Americans were filling the skies with women in bathing suits.

It would take some time for the British to get used to the Americans, and vice versa. But there was a mutual respect, and perhaps more importantly, there was a common enemy. Differences in culture and attitude were quickly set aside as the Allies learned to work together in what would become perhaps the greatest battle of good versus evil in history.

▶ An 8th Air Force B-17 bomber raiding Focke-Wulf plants at Marienburg, Germany, now Malbork, Poland, on October 9, 1943.

PILOT

THE PILOT OF A B-17 didn't just fly the airplane — he was the commander of the whole aircraft, the head of a 10-man crew. Often referred to as "The Skipper" or "The Old Man," the average age of a B-17 pilot in World War II was just 21 years old. That is a lot of responsibility for someone just barely old enough to buy a beer. As an aircraft commander, the pilot was expected to set the tone for the aircraft and inspire the crew to work together. Combat forges unbreakable bonds, and successful bomber crews became closer than brothers, each crew member with a vital role in ensuring the success of a mission. The best commanders led by example.

When you see B-17 pilots in old war movies, they always enter the airplane via the front hatch, pulling themselves up and swinging aboard with an almost artistic flourish. In the movies, it's a macho move and paints a glamorous picture of fearless, square-jawed leaders. When interviewing one B-17 pilot I asked about this, and I'll never forget his response.

"Oh yeah, I know what you mean," he said. "Sure I did it some. That was until we flew our first mission. On our first mission, we were told to stick close to another veteran crew. On that mission, while approaching the target, the veteran crew took a direct flak hit in their bomb bay. They just disappeared into a giant fireball. Debris flew out of the explosion and pieces of their aircraft punctured ours. We flew home with parts of their aircraft sticking out of ours. After a few days we flew another mission, and I knew that my crew was not fully recovered from that ordeal mentally. That morning I entered the aircraft through the hatch back in the waist section of the aircraft. I took a few moments with each man and made sure that I saw them and more importantly they saw me. It was my way of letting them know that we would get through this, and I would do my best to bring them home. And I did. I brought every one of them home 35 times. I consider that my greatest achievement."

HAL WEEKLEY

AS WE BEGIN TALKING about crew members who flew in the B-17 during the war, I can think of no better person to start with than Col. Hal Weekley, a pilot assigned to the 398th Bomb Group, 601st Bomb Squadron. Hal was based at RAF Nuthampstead during the war, and his aircraft carried the triangle W markings on the tail, just like our B-17, *Aluminum Overcast*. Hal was one tough cookie. On one mission his crew had to ditch their airplane. Usually during the war if you didn't make it back to base after a few days, your bunkmates who shared your Quonset hut would go through your personal belongings and take your clean socks, good luck charms, and even love letters. Hal's crew returned after a few weeks. They thought their gear would be long gone. Yet when they arrived everything was still in place. Hal asked, "What gives?" His roommates responded, "You are too tough; we were afraid you might still be alive." His aircraft was nicknamed *Brooklyn Bum* and carried the code letters 30-H on the fuselage, but it had no nose art. The skin around the nose of the aircraft was painted all black, after the Alclad coating was stripped by chemicals used in the enemy's anti-aircraft shells. The ground crews had trouble keeping the nose from corroding, so they painted the nose black. Years later Hal would be an important part of EAA's B-17 Flight Experience program. He not only volunteered with the restoration, but also worked tirelessly to call attention to the importance of the airplane and its mission — to honor and educate. Hal also worked with the 398th Bomb Group Association, which helped finance the restoration. In return, we painted the aircraft in 398th colors and then chose his squadron codes to be represented on the aircraft. For years, you could buy a ride on our B-17 and fly with Hal, an original World War II B-17 pilot. Having flown B-17s during WWII, and then again from 1979 through 2001, he truly lived up to the title of his memoir, *The Last of the Combat B-17 Drivers*.

TIMELESS VOICES

THOMAS HARDIN

WHILE THE MAJORITY of U.S. pilots during the war were officers, Thomas H. Hardin Jr. began his career as one of about 2,500 staff sergeant pilots. He was assigned to the 303rd Bomb Group, 360th Bomb Squadron, which was based at RAF Molesworth. The group was nicknamed "Hell's Angels." Thomas was assigned to the B-17 named *Toy Doll* and was in that aircraft on January 22, 1945, when he was leading a bomber formation. The aircraft was hit by anti-aircraft fire and lost its No. 1 one engine. A mechanical issue prevented Thomas from feathering the propeller, effectively turning that engine into a giant air brake. At this time he also noticed fuel and oil leaking from the No. 2 and 4 engines. He told the crew to start preparing to bail out but hated the idea of his men and him becoming POWs. He decided to continue nursing the aircraft over the English Channel. They were flying at just 120 knots, about 30 knots slower than they should have been. He described the quiet sound inside the big bomber as "spooky." After landing, they counted 200 holes in the airplane. Thomas stayed in the U.S. Air Force, retiring in 1962 as a major, and was awarded a much-belated Distinguished Flying Cross in 2003. He flew on an Old Glory Honor Flight and his family joined us for a flight in June 2013.

▶ While Thomas was at Randolph Field in Texas, he met Maebelle, who was in the Women's Army Corps serving as an air traffic controller. She would often hop rides in AT-6s and once had to bail out. They met in a local club and a short time later they married and enjoyed the rest of their lives together.

DONALD CHRISTENSEN

LT. DONALD "DON" CHRISTENSEN was born in the fall of 1917 in Salt Lake City, Utah, the 13th child of the family. The family soon moved to California, where he spent most of his life. He married a woman named Jocile, whom everyone called "Jo." He worked for Lockheed Vega at the Burbank factory, and when war broke out he was given a deferment. He had applied to become a police officer, and when his application was accepted, he left his job at the factory, which rendered his deferment invalid. After he was told he was going to be drafted, Don enlisted in the U.S. Army Air Forces.

He went through primary training at Twentynine Palms, California, then on to Bakersfield, California, for basic flight training, and Pecos, Texas, for his advanced training. After that, he was assigned to B-17 training in Roswell, New Mexico; Sioux City, Iowa; and Lincoln, Nebraska. Officers were allowed to have their families with them so Jo and his son lived with him on base.

"One day Dad took us out to see his B-17," said Don's son, also named Don. "I remember he carried me out there to the flightline where they were parked. I remember him opening up the rear hatch, and we crawled forward in the airplane. To me as a kid, it seemed like a giant plane. I remember walking through the bomb bay on the catwalk, and there were blue training bombs on the racks in it. Then I had the chance to stand up in the cockpit. Just then another aircraft in the line of bombers started up. It scared me as I thought we were taking off." When he shipped out for England, his family returned to California. His pay didn't cover a house, so Jo and young Don lived with her parents.

When Don arrived in Europe, he, like Hal Weekley, was also assigned to the 398th Bomb Group. He started flying missions with his crew, and when he had time, sent letters back home to his family. As the spring of 1945 rolled around, the German Luftwaffe was all but defeated. It was more in the habit of hiding airplanes than coming after the bomber formations in great numbers. On March 2, 1945, the 398th was flying a mission to Germany. The Luftwaffe had been working on one final desperate push to defend the homeland in the air. The 398th was met with a large fighter resistance, as gaggles of Me 109s and Fw 190s swarmed the attacking bombers. Don's B-17 was experiencing mechanical issues so the flight engineer had to manually operate systems onboard. Their aircraft became a straggler in the formation and was soon trailing behind the rest of the group by about a half-mile. Several Fw 190s made cannon attacks on the rear of Don's aircraft, and the tail was blown off. The tail gunner managed to free himself from the falling aircraft and deployed his parachute. He was the only survivor.

Back home in California, the younger Don was noticing a lot of activity in the house as several of his extended family was soon around a lot. He was not told at first about the loss of his father, as Jo feared he was too young to handle it.

"My mother tried to hide it the best she could, but I could tell something was wrong," he said. "I was later called down to a service being held at the Douglas Aircraft plant at Long Beach. I was told that I would be representing my father and would be presented his Distinguished Flying Cross as well as his Purple Heart. I was 7 years old standing in file with all of these adult servicemen. I kept thinking that just maybe it was all a mistake and that my father would show up."

Years went by before Don started researching his father's service and discovered that a memorial overseas had been built to honor the crew. He also discovered a whole support network to help with the loss he still felt.

"I started attending the 398th Bomb Group Association reunions. I came out to see the *Aluminum Overcast* for a ground tour," he said.

Years later I connected with Don when he got to fly in the cockpit of our B-17, where his father served and ultimately lost his life.

"As I stood there between the pilots, right near where my father would have been, I watched the pilot flying," Don said. "I could just imagine my father there doing it. It was something very special for me."

◀ The two Donolds together, just before the senior Donald Christensen went off to war.

HOWARD KRASEMANN

LT. HOWARD KRASEMANN was a B-17 pilot in the 486th Bomb Group, and he took his B-17, *American Beauty*, aloft on his first mission the day after his 20th birthday. On one of his 33 missions the aircraft was hit by flak. The enemy fire knocked out two of the engines and wounded some of the men on the aircraft. It also shot away Howard's seat. He

▲ This photo from Howard Krasemann's photo album was taken from the tail gunner's position of another B-17, and was saved by Roland Andrews, who helped form the 486th Bomb Group Association.

gave his guys the choice to bail out if they wanted and insisted he would do his best to fly the airplane home for those who could not bail out due to their condition. The entire crew decided to stick together. Once they landed they discovered all of the damage. One of the bursts that had gone off hit the ball turret directly, killing the gunner inside.

"All they could do is literally spray the aircraft down," Howard said. He was awarded an Air Medal and a Bronze Star Medal. His son, Keith Krasemann, flew aboard our aircraft in West Bend, Wisconsin, in 2014.

ED STEVENS

ED STEVENS flew with the 750th Squadron of the 457th Bomb Group, stationed at RAF Glatton. During one of the many daring daylight missions he flew, his aircraft took a direct flak hit just as it crossed the enemy coast. The wings sustained extensive damage, and two engines were knocked out. Ed was one of the

▲ Ed Stevens kneeling at the head of a wounded crew member as he administers first aid.

only members of the crew not wounded. Several members asked him to bail out to save himself, but he refused. Instead, he turned back for home and dove to just 200 feet to evade enemy fighters. He found an airfield and, while on short final, lost a third engine, completing the landing on just one. Having spent time in the medical corps, he immediately started giving his crew first aid. Years later at the age of 92, he was awarded the Silver Star Medal. His daughter, Linda McVeigh Stevens, flew with us in his honor in the summer of 2013 when our B-17 was in Missouri.

PAT PATTERSON

CAPT. PAT PATTERSON of the 388th Bomb Group flew a B-17 named *Princess Pat*. He flew 10 missions as a lieutenant and then became a lead pilot. As a captain, he led the group on 25 more missions. On one mission just prior to engine start, he was asked if he would carry a reporter from *Stars and Stripes*. Years later he discovered this reporter was the famous Andy Rooney of *60 Minutes* fame.

One day, while they were down for repairs, another crew reported that their ball turret gunner had the flu and could not fly. Pat's ball turret gunner volunteered to fill in as they had several friends on this aircraft. On the flight the airplane was shot up, and the ball gunner was stuck in the turret.

"We all went out to watch the planes returning from the day when we saw one B-17 circling off in the distance," Pat said. "Someone from the tower came down and told us that 'your ball turret gunner is in that plane. He is stuck inside, and they can't get the landing gear down. They are trying to figure out what to do.'" They circled for about 30 minutes before they finally had no choice but to land. The ball turret gunner was killed when the airplane made its belly landing.

"There is not a day that goes by that I do not think of him and the sacrifice he made," Pat said. "He just tried to help out his friends. You never really forget something like that."

▲ Pat Patterson back in the cockpit of our B-17. While he didn't actually fly the airplane that day, he remained in the cockpit for the entire flight, and told us that he was ready if we needed him.

On the day that he came to fly with us in May of 2013, Pat's muscle memory took over. Without missing a beat, he climbed up through the forward hatch and slid himself right into his old seat.

ROBERT KILLMARK

ROBERT KILLMARK was a B-17 pilot in the 15th Air Force based in Foggia, Italy. He was sick with the flu on the day of his first scheduled mission and was grounded. His crew went without him, and they did not come back. He had four Fortresses shot out from under him, yet he never got a scratch. They called the cockpit of his aircraft "Killmark's Chapel." His B-17s were all named *Berlin Sleeper* except for a few missions he flew in *G.I. Delivery*. Robert returned to the sky in friendlier times when he flew onboard our B-17 in Brooksville, Florida, in 2015.

DONALD W. STOULIL

DONALD W. STOULIL was a B-17 pilot in the 303rd Bomb Group, 359th Bomb Squadron. He flew this airplane on a January 11 mission that he describes as his worst.

"We lost 50 bombers that day," he said, in a phone call. Every year since the end of the war, his navigator calls him on the date of the mission.

▲ This photograph is a still frame from the documentary *Target for Today*, which was filmed at the 303rd Bomb Group, the "Hell's Angels Squadron." Don Stoulil can be seen just left of center in this photo, and to his right is Vern Moncur.

JAMES CLEM

JAMES CLEM WAS a B-17 pilot in the 15th Air Force, based in Italy. This story came to us through a phone call with one of his family members in September 2014. On his 36th mission, his airplane was severely damaged by flak. He struggled to stay in the air long enough to give his crew a chance to bail out over Yugoslavia. The last guy froze, so James went back and threw him out of the bomb bay. "The longest few seconds of my life were waiting to make sure his chute opened," James said. When James landed, he injured his hip, so a 14-year-old girl helped hide him and collected his chute. With her help, they were smuggled back to Italy. Sixty years later, he was invited back to Croatia to visit. He was taken to where his plane went down, and while there, a 74-year-old woman appeared. It was that 14-year-old girl, 60 years later. She had made her wedding dress out of his parachute.

CLINT HAMMOND

LT. CLINT HAMMOND flew 30 missions in the 351st Bomb Group. On his third mission, heading to Munich, as they approached the target he saw what looked like a dark storm front coming. It turned out to be a wall of flak.

"As we started our bomb run my co-pilot fainted from fear," he said. "The top turret gunner came down and took care of him. When we landed and crawled out of the plane I took my gloves off and punched him out. You have to understand, there was a lot at stake, and I was responsible for all of their lives."

JIM STOPULOS

LT. JIM STOPULOS was a B-17 pilot in the 94th Bomb Group, 332nd Bomb Squadron. He flew 29 missions, including two on D-Day.

▲ Jim Stopulos (front row, kneeling, far left) and his crew, with whom he flew 29 missions.

"When we got up in the air, there were more airplanes than I'd ever seen in my life! It almost blotted out the sun," he said. "When we got over the English Channel, it was covered with boats, an amazing sight I'll never forget. I knew that the odds were against us surviving our missions. I had this defense mechanism to help me think through the mission. I would tell my one friend to get a card game going for that night. That was my little way of planning to be back that night." When he was 99 years old, he wanted to make one more run in the B-17, and he did that with us in Davenport, Iowa.

JOHN CORCORAN

LT. JOHN CORCORAN flew a B-17 named *Gloria Ann* in the 390th Bomb Group. The airplane was named after his fiancée back home. He is seen here inspecting damage to his aircraft after it returned with more than 700 holes shot in it. John came out to fly with us in 2014, and then his son flew with us two years later.

RICHARD GILLESPIE

CAPT. RICHARD GILLESPIE was a B-17 pilot in the 447th Bomb Group. After being noticed for flying tight formations, he was made a lead pilot. He then was given a B-17 with an H2X "Mickey" radar unit in it and led the group. He flew 23 missions and was awarded the Distinguished Flying Cross for bombing an Me 262 plant and scoring a direct hit. He and his family flew with us in Clearwater, Florida, in 2014.

▲ A close-up of *Gloria Ann's* nose art.

◄ Richard flying the B-17 *Miss Lace* of the 447th Bomb Group.

WILLIAM H. LONG

LT. WILLIAM H. LONG flew both B-24s and B-17s in the 486th Bomb Group. He flew 35 missions during WWII. His daughter Nancy came out to visit the B-17 on a tour stop in September 2015.

"A new crew joined his squadron, and since he had flown a few missions, he was asked to train them," she said. "He flew a few practice missions with them. On the new crew's first mission out, they were hit by flak and went down. All William could do is watch helplessly from his bomber."

CHUCK CHILDS

CHUCK CHILDS FLEW a B-17 named *Gravel Gertie*, and he flew with us at EAA AirVenture Oshkosh.

"I never had an easy mission," he said. "I lost a top turret gunner and a waist gunner. I once flew home over 600 miles on two engines. On short final the third engine gave up. I ended up landing on one engine. As we rolled out, it coughed and stopped."

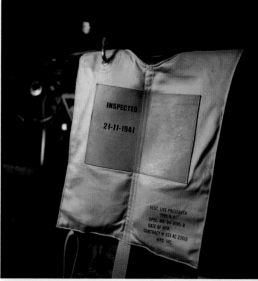

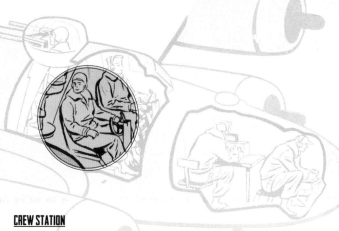

CO-PILOT

TO SOME, THE JOB of co-pilot might seem less than glamorous, sitting in the right seat in the cockpit next to a command pilot who is in charge of everything. However, that could not be further from the truth. B-17 co-pilots were trained and qualified just the same as the pilots. They were fully rated pilots, and they knew the aircraft's systems inside and out. Moreover, more times than not, a co-pilot would eventually get his own crew. During the early missions in 1942 and 1943 the 8th Air Force would turn a co-pilot into an aircraft commander after just a few missions as they were facing a high loss rate. Famed *Memphis Belle* co-pilot Jim Verinis told a group of new crews, "You co-pilots, don't plan on getting to England and staying a co-pilot for very long." The truth is that the B-17 was a complex aircraft for its time. In fact, when the Model 299 first rolled out, many felt that it was too complex to fly. As crews began flying the B-17 in combat, the need for a co-pilot became clear. Having two pilots up front was critical as the bombers started taking heavy losses. A second pilot meant the ability to continue flying the airplane even if one was injured. On many occasions the bombers returned with only one pilot flying the aircraft, and in many cases with both pilots wounded. It was the teamwork between both pilots that made the aircraft successful in their missions.

JOHN "LUCKY" LUCKADOO

JOHN "LUCKY" LUCKADOO was born and raised in Chattanooga, Tennessee. This is where he was driving some neighborhood kids around in his car when they heard on the radio that Pearl Harbor had been bombed.

"I remember that we were all trying to figure out where the heck Pearl Harbor was," he said. Like so many, he decided he wanted to join the military. In January of 1942, when he was 19, Lucky and his best friend Sullivan went to join.

"They said they would take us but that there were so many people joining we would have to wait around until March," he said. "We had thought about joining the RCAF. I decided to go the USAAF route and joined, being placed on leave until March. Sullivan would join the RCAF and go on to fly Spitfires as well as later the Typhoon." In March the training began, and Lucky went from base to base as he went through the progression of higher-performance aircraft.

"I was probably the only guy in the Air Forces who never had to go to Texas for training somehow," he said. Lucky was assigned as a B-17 co-pilot. "In February of 1943 we were ordered to Salt Lake City. Once there, something happened which would really take us all by surprise." A decision was made to replace all of the group's co-pilots with a recently graduated class of 40 multiengine pilots from Moody Field in Valdosta, Georgia.

"We now had fresh co-pilots in the right seats who have never sat in a B-17 before," he said. "We were assigned to the 100th Bomb Group and given orders to fly to Europe. Little did any of us know at the time that of the 40 classmates, only four of us would make it through our tour of 25 missions." When he began the Atlantic crossing, via the northern route, Lucky had just 20 hours in the B-17.

"We were stuck for two weeks in Newfoundland waiting for the right winds. While we were there our pilot made the mistake of getting involved with a WAAF, a British gal in the military," he said. "He became hospitalized with VD, and we had to wait for him to get out of the hospital. Once he did, he was too weak to fly. We loaded up, and I flew us the rest of the way to England. I had 50 hours' total time in the B-17 at this point."

Once they arrived in England, Lucky and the 100th were assigned to RAF Thorpe Abbotts.

"They sent a training mission out just to give a few of the guys some practice. They carried no bombs or guns on the mission," he said. "It was just meant to be a formation exercise and stay fairly local. They wandered out over the Channel, and the Germans found them and jumped them. We lost three planes and 30 men on nothing more than just a training flight.

"I was a member of the original group. We flew our first combat mission on June 25, 1943. Each mission would start the same

▲ John Luckadoo in front of his PT-17 Stearman trainer.

way," Lucky said. "They would wake us up around 3 a.m., or sometimes we could sleep in until 3:30 a.m. depending on where we were going. You would have a short period of time to get a shower and dressed. Then down to breakfast. Then to briefing. This would be the first time you would find out where you were going. You would also learn about the target, rally points, and any type of escort we might have. We usually had nothing in the way of fighter escort. Sometimes the RAF would send some Spitfires up the coast to meet us. They would run low on fuel and go and refuel, then try to get us on our way home if we survived.

"After briefing we would go out to the planes and prepare for takeoff. We would usually take off before dawn. Most of the time we had a low overcast. So we would be making basically instrument takeoffs and then immediately pull up into the soup," he

said. As you can imagine it was a dangerous operation with this many airplanes, heavily loaded, trying to bite into the air.

"Once in a while you would see a big glow in the fog at the end of the runway. That is how you would know that someone had gone in on takeoff," he said. Another hazardous part of the mission was simply forming up.

"There was an airfield of some sort every 5 miles in England," he said. "So you would have multiple groups trying to take off and form up all at once. We had a pattern we were supposed to follow, but sometimes folks would stray from that and there would be a collision. We had a lot of those."

As Lucky climbed to altitude it got colder and colder in the airplane.

"We would climb up to about 26,000 to 29,000 feet. That is where we normally operated from. The temperature would be about minus 50 to minus 60 degrees Fahrenheit onboard the aircraft," he said. As they neared the target, tensions mounted on the crew as they knew the enemy was coming for them.

"On my first mission, we turned on the IP, or initial point to the target, and were walled with flak. It was so thick you could put the gear down and taxi on it," he said. "By the time we reached our target we had lost 12 out of the 18 aircraft we started in with."

I asked Lucky if there was a particularly hard mission that stood out for him. Without hesitation, he immediately responded with one word, "Bremen."

"September 16, 1943, it was my 21st mission. Bremen was the first time I saw the German fighters so hell bent on getting us that they flew through their own flak," he said. "Two Fw 190s lined up out in front of us and came in head on at us. The flight lead became so focused on knocking us down that he rammed the B-17 next to us named *Piccadilly Lilly*. I had to pitch the nose down, and the plane coming after us went right over us and actually nicked our top turret. We were still flying in the temperature of minus 50 to minus 60 Fahrenheit, but the difference is that in combat you were still sweating. Then it would freeze and jam your oxygen mask. So you would have to try to break up the ice in your mask with one hand, and fly the plane with the other. The Germans were a very skilled enemy. They had a lot of practice prior to us getting there."

Lucky found himself as the last lead pilot still flying after the bombs were away and fired a flare for everyone to form up on him.

"My aircraft had taken damage. A flak burst hit the nose, shattering all of the glass. The burst was so intense that it blew the

▲ John Luckadoo and William DeSanders after the completion of another mission.

a rookie crew. This was their first mission. This is how the 100th Bomb Group came to be known as 'The Bloody 100th.'"

When asked if he was afraid on the missions, Lucky said that you just couldn't think about it.

"Keep yourself busy. If you thought about it, you might fall apart," he said. "I had a ball turret gunner who wet himself during combat. He froze to the turret. We tried to get him out of there and could not. So I had to land with him in the turret. Something very dangerous as others had lost a gunner trapped in there before. We landed on the grass, and they had to chip him out of the turret. Once in the hospital he was told that he was going to be awarded the Purple Heart. He said, 'Oh no! I don't want to have to tell people how I got this!'"

Lucky's best friend Sullivan, who had gone on to fly in the RCAF, once stopped in to visit him with a Spitfire. Lucky took Sullivan up for a B-17 flight, and Sullivan said that it felt like driving a truck. Sullivan then let him fly his Spitfire.

"I was worried it was too much plane for me, but he said it was easy, so I gave it a try," Lucky said. "It was a very smooth airplane. A few weeks later, I had to take a B-17 out on a maintenance flight, so I decided to stop by Sullivan's base and surprise him." Lucky landed his big bomber on the runway at the RAF base, and as he taxied in he went by the wreckage of a burned-out fighter.

"I thought nothing of it. Once parked the RAF folks came out to see me," he said. "'Are you lost, Yank?'" they asked him. Lucky replied that he was looking for his friend. They led him to the commanding officer's quarters. The CO asked how he knew Sullivan, and Lucky replied that Sullivan was his best friend.

"Quietly, the CO explained that the wreckage I saw coming in was Sullivan," Lucky said. "His engine failed on takeoff, and he cartwheeled down the runway." The CO asked if Lucky would write the letter home. He was not sure if he could. Eventually, Lucky wrote the letter to Sullivan's mother explaining what happened. She had lost a husband in World War I, and now her only son in World War II.

Lucky flew 25 missions, which was a full tour of duty at that time. These missions were between eight and 10 hours.

"After flying these missions, we would land just completely physically and emotionally exhausted," he said. "Sometimes we wouldn't be able to stand. Sometimes we would just sit in the plane for a few minutes and regain our composure."

bombardier back into the tunnel," he said. "So the cold wind was ripping through the aircraft. My feet were frozen to the rudder pedals. We had lost an engine so I was trying my best to keep up the speed. After the day was done, we had lost seven of the 18 planes we departed with. They would have to chip my feet from the rudder pedals. I would spend the next few days in the hospital, and this probably saved my life. The next day the 100th went out with another 18 planes. This time nine came home. The day after that they were told that the mission was max effort. So anything or one who could fly the mission had to go. They sent out another 18 planes. This time one came home. The crew that made it home was

My time with Lucky was special. During my talk at EAA AirVenture Oshkosh, he and his godson turned up in the audience. I felt foolish giving a talk about life onboard a B-17 with the real deal in attendance. Afterward he came up and answered questions from the crowd with me. After, almost by fate, a co-worker called and asked if I knew of anyone wanting to fly on the B-17 as we had two empty seats. Lucky and his godson got the chance to fly together.

"It is a much different experience flying in one for fun," Lucky said. "It is warm, and no one is shooting at me. It brings back a lot of memories.

"War is really a folly. There are no winners; we all lose," he said. "No one wins when we send young people off to die. I hope that we learn from the past and learn that wars are not the way. As for me? Somehow, I got through my 25 missions in the Bloody 100th. Whether you lived or died had nothing to do with skill. It was all luck. That is why I always say they should have nicknamed me 'Darn Lucky!'"

▲ John Luckadoo (kneeling, far right) and the crew of *Sunny II.*

DOUG HOLT

DOUG HOLT STARTED as a co-pilot with the 92nd Bomb Group when he was just 19, and then he was moved up to pilot and even lead pilot. I was able to spend a great weekend with him as we sold rides for the B-17 at an air show in Waukesha, Wisconsin. While we were there he shared some of his stories. His B-17 was named *Lucky Dog,* and he later used that for the title of his book.

"I was too short to climb in through the front hatch in the nose of our Fortress," he said. "So my crew would pick me up and hoist me through the entryway." Years later, when EAA was first given the B-17, Doug was a major volunteer and supporter, and he spent a lot of time working on the old bomber to restore it to its current condition. It is because of dedicated volunteers like Doug and so many countless others that our aircraft looks as good as it does today.

TIMELESS VOICES

RICHARD BENDER

RICHARD WAS A CO-PILOT in the 447th Bomb Group. During one of his missions, his airplane was hit by German flak. Seven out of the 10 crew members were able to bail out of the aircraft and became POWs until the end of the war. While we were in Ashville, North Carolina, in October 2013, Richard's granddaughter, Jody Bender, flew with us and experienced firsthand what life was like onboard a B-17.

▲ Richard was eventually shot down in this B-17.

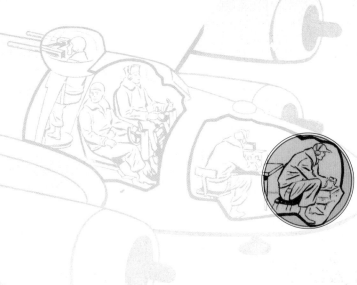

BOMBARDIER

THE BOMBARDIER'S ROLE was crucial to the mission of the B-17 — dropping bombs on target to destroy the enemy's ability to wage war. The bombardier sat farthest forward in the aircraft, in the glass nose section. He had the best view in the house, until that view was filled with German fighters and anti-aircraft fire. He was responsible for arming the bombs on the aircraft as well as making sure they were secure for the mission. His other responsibility was the Norden bombsight, one of the war's biggest and best-kept secrets. It was said the Norden bombsight could put a bomb in a pickle barrel from 30,000 feet. While on the final leg of the bomb run, the bombardier flew the Fortress through an autopilot that was slaved to the bombsight. The final duty the bombardier had was that of a gunner when the aircraft was not on the bomb run. On earlier models of the B-17, the bombardier manned a single .50-caliber machine gun in the nose, while late F models and all G models were equipped with chin turrets armed with twin .50-caliber machine guns.

ROBERT F. SCHNEIDER

ROBERT F. SCHNEIDER was a bombardier assigned to the 351st Bomb Group based at RAF Polebrook. He was credited with scoring a direct hit on the target they were bombing from 30,000 feet. He then became a lead bombardier. His B-17 was named *Miss Glamour Pants*. When the time came for us to pull together our Freedom Flight, which is covered in more detail in Chapter 22, he was our choice to represent bombardiers. He lived just north of EAA headquarters in Green Bay, Wisconsin. When the day came, we were surprised by the fact that among his family was former Green Bay Packers head coach Mike McCarthy. The families had time to explore the B-17 before the flight, and I will always cherish the memory of Robert explaining to his teenage great-granddaughter, who was sitting in his old seat, what all of the switches did on the bombardier panel.

TIMELESS VOICES

▲ Robert Schneider gazing at his old office during a 2013 visit to our aircraft during winter maintenance.

FLOYD HENDERSHOT

FLOYD HENDERSHOT served as a bombardier on a B-17 named *Ready Freddie* in the 95th Bomb Group. When his daughter flew with us, she said, "He never talked about it much. He served on B-36s and B-52s as well. But never talked about WWII with us. We later found out that he was awarded a Distinguished Flying Cross for leading his group on a mission on D-Day."

▲ Floyd (third from right) with his crew in front of their B-17, *Ready Freddie*.

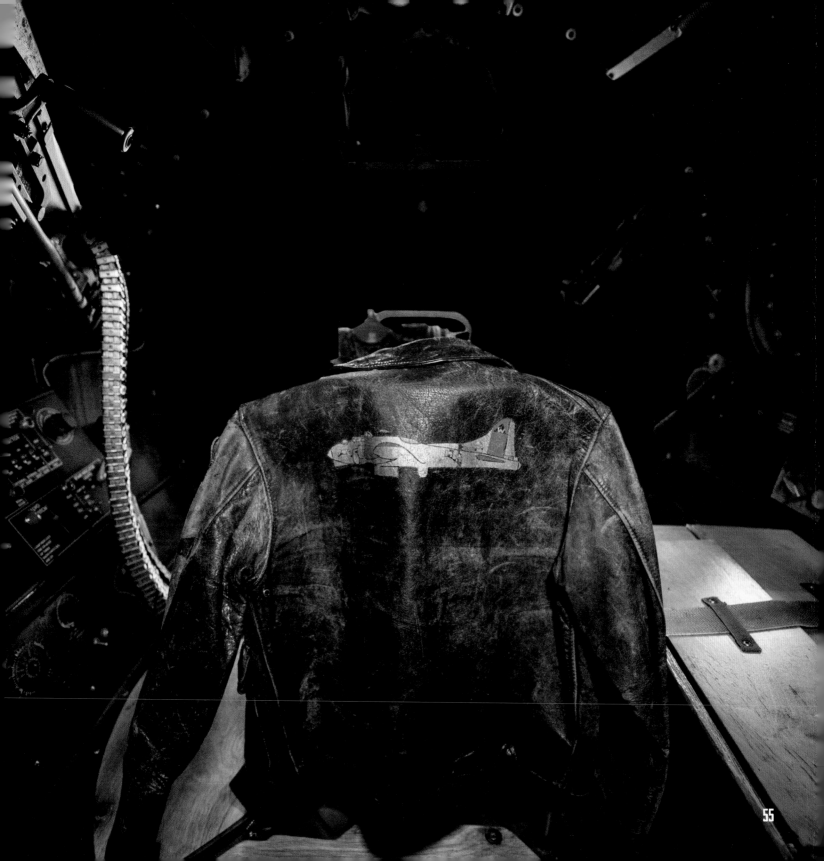

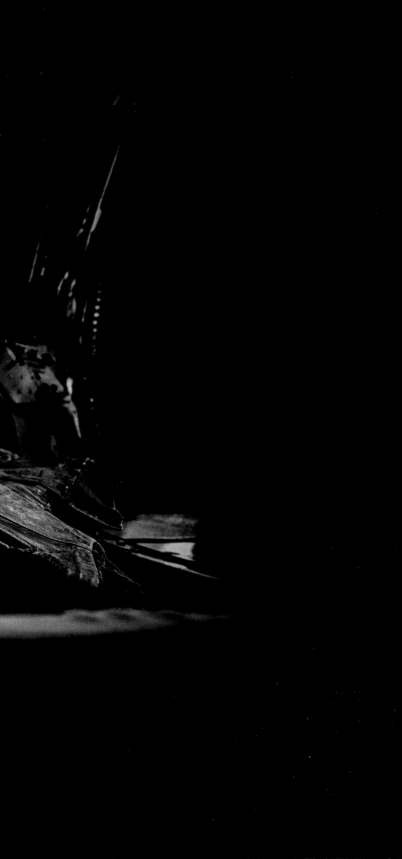

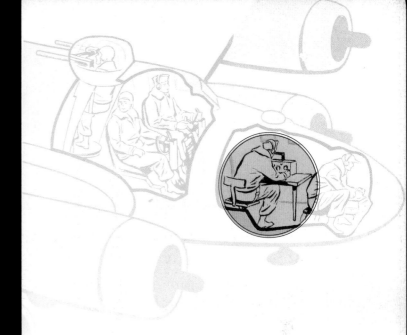

NAVIGATOR

WHEN YOU CLIMB into a B-17, it's not hard to identify the navigator's position, as his table was in the nose of the aircraft, behind the bombardier on the left side. The navigator was in charge of keeping the aircraft on course, and therefore was highly trained in navigation for both day and night and in all weather. He had to know how to plot courses and use a sextant to shoot the stars, a slang term for using celestial navigation. The first true test for most of the navigators was finding their way from the United States to the theater of combat. Prior to a mission they would be given a briefing with checkpoints, and it was up to the navigator to ensure the aircraft was on course and on target, giving the bombardier his best shot. He also usually had a gun to man when not taking fixes or evaluating the B-17's location and course.

ROBERT BURKART

ONE SUMMER WEEKEND we flew the B-17 up to the Green Bay, Wisconsin, airport for ground tours and ride experiences. I noticed a couple sitting and talking as they viewed the aircraft from afar. The gentleman was wearing a hat with the 398th Bomb Group insignia, the same group that our B-17 commemorates with its paint scheme. I approached the couple and asked if he had served in the war.

"Oh yes, I sure did," he said. "I was a navigator in the B-17 in the 398th Bomb Group."

The more we talked, the more amazing details I learned about the missions he flew. But he left one thing out. Robert wasn't just a navigator; he was a lead navigator. He was one of the guys who was so good at his job that the squadron placed all of its faith in his abilities and followed him into hostile skies.

▲ Marion Burkart watches as her husband, Robert, departs in our B-17 for one more mission in Green Bay, Wisconsin.

"I keep trying to get him to sign up for one of the Honor Flights, but he won't do it," his wife, Marion, said. I asked him why he did not want to go on the Honor Flight. His response was very matter of fact. "I don't feel that I deserve it," he said. "I didn't do anything to warrant any kind of special treatment like that."

DONALD MUSTON

SECOND LT. DONALD MUSTON was a B-17 navigator in the 457th Bomb Group. While on a mission on June 14, 1944, to Le Bourget, France, his aircraft was struck by anti-aircraft fire. An explosion violently rocked the aircraft, knocking him out cold. The airplane was going down, and everyone had only a matter of seconds to bail out. His friend, the bombardier, dragged him to the escape hatch and threw him out. He was reunited with the B-17 when he and his son flew with us aboard *Aluminum Overcast* at a tour stop in Redding, California.

▲ Bombs away! Donald is in the center B-17 as his flight unloads on the target.

BOB SPRAIGHT

"I WAS DATING A GIRL named Joyce before the war," said Bob Spraight, a B-17 navigator, when we met at the EAA Aviation Museum in Oshkosh. "There was nothing not to like about her. She was beautiful and had this amazing voice. She sang in a coloratura soprano voice that was just so pretty. She and I along with some friends would go down to the lake on a boat to the Lake Austin Inn. When I found out that I was assigned to bombers in the 8th Air Force I broke it off. A ticket to the 8th Air Force in those days was about the same as a death certificate. I didn't think I had a chance in hell I'd make it back. I didn't want her going through all of that."

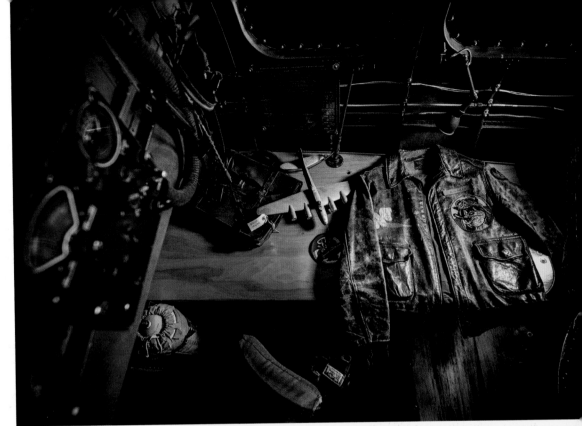

EXPERIENCE
ALUMINUM
Overcast

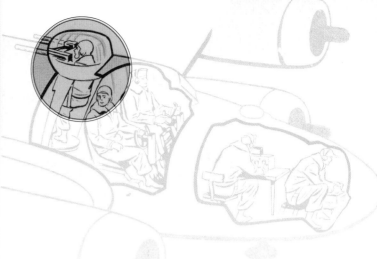

TOP TURRET

THE TOP TURRET was a plexiglass dome on top of the fuselage just aft of the cockpit, and it was equipped with twin .50-caliber machine guns. The gunner who manned this position was also the aircraft's flight engineer. When he wasn't manning the guns to protect the aircraft from attack from above, he was assisting the pilot, monitoring the engines and other systems to ensure the B-17 was in good working order. When the aircraft was on the ground he helped oversee repairs and maintenance, always ensuring his aircraft was fit to fly the next mission. Flight engineers were even trained and equipped to make simple repairs as needed.

GEORGE E. FREITAG

GEORGE E. FREITAG was a top turret gunner in the 483rd Bomb Group. They were on a bomb run when a massive flak burst hit their aircraft, a burst that was so violent that the pilot later remarked that he thought it had loosened the left wing. The bomb racks and catwalks were partially destroyed. George's friend, the radio operator, Thomas Lewicki, was wounded and his parachute destroyed. Knowing that it was going to be a long ride home for a wounded gunner, and in an effort to keep him fighting, George took his own parachute off and threw it out of the window, saying that if his friend couldn't bail out, he wouldn't either. The crew fought to keep the aircraft in the air and get it back to a base. Upon landing, the crew had parachutes tied to the waist gun mounts to try to slow it down. After the mission the base's commanding officer went out and counted the holes. He stopped at 30,748. That stands today as an Air Force record for the most heavily damaged aircraft to return from a mission. There is a memorial for the aircraft calling this out at the Museum of Aviation at Warner Robins, Georgia. A family member of George's told us this story while we were in Illinois in the fall of 2013.

▶ The series of photos on the right shows the extensive damage to the aircraft.

FRANK GRAMENZI

TECH SGT. FRANK GRAMENZI was the top turret gunner on a B-17 named *MIZPAH*. On July 14, 1944, the aircraft took a direct flak hit in the nose. Despite losing the whole nose and windshield area, the pilots managed to keep it in the air long enough to give the crew a chance to bail out. In the fall of 2013, Frank's granddaughter, Rochelle, flew with us and had a chance to see a part of her grandfather's life firsthand.

▲ Staff Sgt. Jack Levine of East Nassau, New York, preparing his turret for another mission with the 324th Bomb Squadron, 91st Bomb Group, in June 1943. He was on the crew of *Our Gang* and had two confirmed enemy aircraft destroyed. He survived the war and returned to New York.

▲ The B-17 *MIZPAH*, with its nose blown off, drops back out of formation, before the crew bailed out.

▲ Chuck Ormsby, a top turret gunner/flight engineer of the 398th Bomb Group, 603rd Bomb Squadron, is standing in the back row at far right. At the time this photo was taken, he was just 24 years old. He went on to fly 35 missions.

LORAN HEEB

TECH SGT. LORAN HEEB was a top turret gunner and flight engineer in the 447th Bomb Group, serving aboard a B-17 known as *Ol' Scrapiron*. The airplane was named in honor of their first pilot, Lt. Robert Stevenson, a mild-mannered, easygoing person who one evening was pushed too far by a bunch of rowdy service personnel. He singlehandedly cleaned house. After this event the officers called him "Ol' Scrapiron." Unfortunately, Stevenson was killed on the first mission out. When Lt. Dahlgran, the original co-pilot, became command pilot he asked for his original crew back, and they voted to name the airplane *Ol' Scrapiron*.

Loran went on to fly a total of 30 missions and died in 2000, but his memory is not forgotten, as his son, Steve, works hard to preserve it.

"He was my best friend," Steve said. "We would go to air shows and he would talk about all of the aircraft that were there, but never talked about himself."

Steve flew with us in Seattle on an anniversary of D-Day, a special day for him as on June 6, 1944, his father was up there flying two combat sorties.

"It was really special to know that I was going up in a B-17 with WWII vets on a date as significant as that," he said. The 447th was based at RAF Rattlesden during the war, and Steve honored his father's legacy even further when he named his son Mitchell Rattlesden Heeb. Steve and Mitchell regularly attend reunions to help ensure that Loran and the crew of *Ol' Scrapiron* will never be forgotten.

▲ Many times families who fly with us bring photos and mementos from their loved ones to take one more flight. Here we see photos of Loran Heeb resting inside of our B-17 during a visit from Steve Heeb, who flew with us.

MIRWOOD STARKEY

TECH SGT. MIRWOOD STARKEY was a top turret gunner in the 452nd Bomb Group. His daughter sent me a copy of his diary. This is the entry from his next-to-last mission.

"The last mission we flew for the Battle of the Bulge. Three holes in the plane," Mirwood wrote. "They hit Olson, our navigator, in the jugular vein. We took the next day off and went to the Cambridge American Cemetery for his funeral. Then we got drunk."

TIMELESS VOICES

RADIO OPERATOR

THE RADIO ROOM on the B-17 is aft of the bomb bay, under a hatch that looks like a skylight. The radio operator was responsible for both air-to-air and air-to-ground communications, usually via Morse code. He sat at a table and would keep records of the mission as well. On some variants of the B-17, that hatch above him would have a single .50-caliber machine gun mounted in it that he used as part of the bomber's defense.

HARVIN ABRAHAMSON

SGT. HARVIN ABRAHAMSON was a radio operator in the 487th Bomb Group. He flew several of his missions on *Miss Bea Havin* as well as *Fearless Fosdick*.

"If you were a replacement crew, you would always deliver a gleaming new airplane just to have it taken away and get handed a beat-up old ship," Harvin said. The new aircraft would be handed over to veteran crews with high mission totals. "I was just happy to be assigned to a B-17 outfit. I did not want to go into a B-24 unit. We used to have a joke that if you yelled flak, the wings of a B-24 would fall off. Our days would start around 2:30 a.m. or 3 a.m. They would come in and wake you up with flashlights or turn on all of the lights in your Quonset hut. I would get ready, then go over and get breakfast."

The military was never known for great food, and Harvin didn't disagree.

"They would give us a breakfast that consisted of powdered eggs, some kind of crummy pancakes, and coffee," he said. "We used to joke that you could hear the pancakes splash in your stomach when they hit the coffee. We sometimes would have milk, but it too was powdered."

Harvin remembered a time when the food caused headlines at the base.

"We had a horrible breakfast, and then all went out to the plane for a mission," he said. "We had just gotten new flak helmets, but for some reason the old ones were still in the plane as well. I told the ground crew that when we returned we would need to get rid of the old ones. As we were en route to the target, which was Berlin, the tail gunner called up over the intercom and said that he needed to move his bowels and asked us to pass him back one of the helmets to use. So we did. His stomach was not right that day as he needed a few helmets. Then the ball turret gunner and one waist gunner also had to. As we reached the bomb run, the bomb bay doors opened, and once more our poor tail gunner needed another helmet. When the bombs dropped we threw them all out. The next day we went by the announcement board where news was posted about the 487th. The headline simply said, 'Tail gunner shits on Berlin.'

"After breakfast we would head over to briefing," Harvin said. "There we would find out where we were going. You really did not want to hear certain town names called out. Something like Berlin had over a thousand anti-aircraft guns around it. After briefing we would pile into jeeps and trucks and head out to the aircraft.

"On our first mission we were assigned to sit alert and fill in in case of another aircraft having a problem," he said. "They would turn back, and we would take off to take their place while the formation was still forming up. Well, we got the call to launch and never were able to catch up to the squadron. So we just found another bomb group and latched onto them and flew the mission with them. We ended up bombing Dresden as the tail-end Charlie to the group."

Harvin had a deal with the bombardier that after the bombs were dropped, he would open the door and check to verify that all of the ordnance had been released. On one mission near Berlin, Harvin opened the door and found a single 500-pounder stuck in the bomb bay. With the doors still open, and lugging a walk-around bottle of oxygen, he went out on the catwalk and tried to kick the bomb free. When that did not work, the bombardier came back with a screwdriver. They both laid on the catwalk, and Harvin held the back of the bombardier's jacket as he worked the bomb free.

On one mission near Berlin, Harvin would have his luck tested.

"We had gotten out of the target area and were heading for home," he said. "I took off my flak helmet and vest and was sitting at my table. We flew over an uncharted flak gun, and it targeted us. The shell came through the floor and hit the steel post my chair was mounted to right between my legs. I started to say my prayers, and another piece of flak hit the compartment ceiling and went right by my head. I then lit up a cigarette."

▲ Harvin (kneeling in the front row, second from right) and his crewmates.

▲ Larry "Goldie" Goldstein at his station at the radio operator's table in his B-17, *Worry Wart*, of the 388th Bomb Group in 1944 (top), and again in our B-17 in 2013 (left).

ALLEN CHANDLER

FERN BRIDGES called me with a powerful story I will never forget. Her husband, Tech Sgt. Allen Chandler, was assigned to the 91st Bomb Group as a radio operator. Before shipping out overseas he knew he had to leave Fern, who was pregnant at the time, at home. He was worried about what would happen to her if he didn't make it back. He didn't want her to be alone in that situation, so he had her move in with his parents. He also had his parents listed as the next of kin so that if something did happen, the military would notify them, and then they could break it to Fern. The day she saw Allen off was the last time they saw one another.

On November 2, 1944, Allen was flying on a B-17 named *Bomber Dear*. Their target was the town of Merseburg, Germany. Flak hit the aircraft and set it on fire, and then it was attacked by enemy fighters. The pilot ordered everyone to bail out, and the airplane crashed at Barby, Germany. Six of the men died in the crash while the others became prisoners of war. It was not long before the Chandler home in Oklahoma received the telegram that Allen was listed as missing in action. He was never found.

After a few years Fern remarried, but she was worried about having to tell Allen's parents. After she told them, Allen's father told her they were glad she wouldn't go on being alone. Upon hearing that powerful story, we asked Fern to fly with us. She sat in Allen's seat in the radio room, where the crew had placed a wartime photo of Allen. Then she went for a ride and experienced what it was like

▲ Parents-to-be Fern and Allen share a lighthearted moment shortly before he shipped out. "I walked him to the train station, and he stopped a few times on the way," she said. "I knew he was scared, and he had a feeling he was not coming back."

▲ Fern Bridges came to see our B-17 and where Allen had served. We surprised her and took her flying. A photo of Allen's aircraft was set up at the radio operator's table.

to be up in a B-17 where Allen had worked. She called me that evening and told me how that was the closest she had felt to him in a long time. I posted a photo and a small write-up of the day, as I did with most of our veterans who flew. A few weeks later the Bomb Group Association contacted me. It was looking for Fern. The Defense POW/MIA Accounting Agency had located the crash site of the aircraft and wanted to contact all family. After a long wait, we received word from Fern that Allen's remains had been identified and were coming home to be buried at Arlington National Cemetery.

"I feel good knowing that we will know where he is," Fern said. That closure was 73 years in the making. On June 27, 2018, Fern and her family attended the service where Allen was laid to rest in Arlington National Cemetery.

"I always thought, please, if he is ever going to come home, let it be while I am still alive," she said. "I am just happy I was here to see it."

▲ Long overdue, Allen, along with the rest of his crew, came home. An honor guard at Arlington National Cemetery hands Fern the burial flag in May 2018.

▲ Morris Spielberg and his crew in the 91st Bomb Group. He flew 35 missions as a radio operator on the B-17 *Zootie Cutie.* "On one mission, we were hit over Germany," he told me. "The pilot worked hard to get it out of harm's way. The '17 was built tough. We made it out to a point where we decided to ditch. Our pilot put it down just as smooth as ever on the water, and we all got out. Great water landing; even that Sully guy would have been proud."

▲ Ray Miner was a radio operator in the 401st Bomb Group. He was on a mission over Châteauroux, France, when a shell exploded in his compartment. They were under fighter attack, and none of the other crew could leave their guns to treat his wounds. Therefore, he treated the wounds himself before going back to his station. He then blacked out, and when he came to, he was being lifted out of the airplane back at their base in England. He was just 19 years old.

DONALD CAMP

TECH SGT. DONALD CAMP was a B-17 radio operator in the 15th Air Force based in Foggia, Italy. He was drafted right out of his Ocala, Florida, high school at 18 years old. He went on to fly 17 bombing missions over heavily defended enemy territory.

"When flak would hit the belly [of] our aircraft it sounded like shotgun BB's," he said. During the war, a crew member assigned to take pictures of Berlin after a bombing refused to go when concern for sufficient fuel was raised and the assignment was deemed a suicide mission by a fellow crew member. Donald took on the assignment.

In January 2015, EAA Chapter 812 hosted a B-17 tour stop in Ocala, Florida. Despite the cold morning, Donald was joined at the bomber by his entire family, all wrapped in jackets and blankets to see him fly what would become his 18th mission. His wife, Christine, sat with him in the aircraft for a few minutes holding his hand. They met on a blind date in 1947 and had been married for 66 years. After a few minutes, she made her way out of the rear hatch as it was time to start the engines. He made his way back to his radio operator station. There in his old seat he peered out of the window to his left, the same window that he looked out of years ago. This time, with no one shooting at him, he was able to simply sit back and enjoy the view. After the 30-minute flight, he got out of the aircraft and was immediately hugged by his grandchildren.

▲ Donald Camp back in his old office on a cold day in Florida.

Ten days later I received a phone call from his daughter — Donald had died.

▲ Donald Camp being greeted by his family after his final mission.

"He was very proud of getting to fly one more time," his daughter said. "It seemed to renew his youth." She later told me that on the way to the hospital he told the paramedics that he got to go up in a B-17 one more time. Donald Camp's story stands out to me as a clear example of the importance of what we do with our B-17. It's far more than just a ride in an old airplane; it's the embodiment of a legacy, one that it is our humble privilege to uphold.

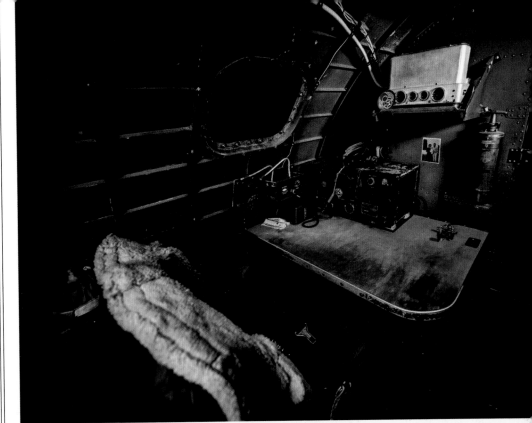

On the National
Defense Front

BALL TURRET

THE BALL TURRET GUNNER is probably one of the most fabled positions on the crew of a B-17. The glass and metal sphere is suspended from under the aircraft and armed with twin .50-caliber machine guns. Prior to the war, most bombers used handheld machine guns in these positions. Early model B-17s had a bulging glass blister in this position up until the C model. The C and D models had a fixture called the bathtub that housed twin .50-caliber machine guns, but they were still handheld. The first E models had a remote-controlled Bendix lower turret. This was hard to aim, and later E models switched to the new electrically operated Sperry ball turret. Someone, usually the shortest member of the crew, had to climb inside this turret and operate it. This position allowed for a great view of the formation, and everything else if you were brave enough to do it. The claustrophobic confines of the turret meant that only the smallest gunners were able to squeeze in while wearing their parachutes — the rest simply left their chutes inside the aircraft.

DEAN LARSON

EARL & MELVIN SERVICE

DEAN LARSON was the ball turret gunner on a B-17 named *Max Effort*. After 15 missions, Dean was wounded when flak hit his ball turret. He was given the opportunity to go home but elected to stay on and finish with his crew. We flew Dean as well as many of his family members onboard the B-17. One of our most special flights was when Dean was no longer able to get out to the airport to see the B-17. We had his great-grandson climb aboard, and we flew him over Dean's assisted living community. He was able to see not only his old airplane once more, but also his legacy living on with his great-grandson.

WHEN PAM RECKELHOFF climbed in our B-17 in Cincinnati in September 2013, she was representing not one but two veterans. Her father, Melvin Service, and her uncle, Earl Service, both served in the 301st Bomb Group, 32nd Bomb Squadron. Melvin served as a cook while his brother Earl was off flying missions in the ball turret of his B-17, *Leadfoot*. On October 30, 1943, during a mission to bomb a ball bearing factory in Turin, Italy, *Leadfoot* developed an engine problem. As the aircraft was heading down, all men managed to parachute out. When air-sea rescue arrived, it could not find any of the crew. All onboard were presumed lost. When Pam flew with us, her uncle's photo was displayed next to the ball turret.

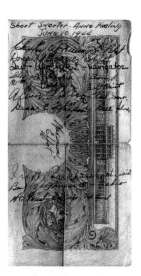

▲ Roger Larson with his family when they flew with us.

▲ Dean Larson's short snorter. A short snorter was any kind of currency that was signed by a group who had flown together. This was common practice during the war and served as a keepsake and good luck charm. Many times, as in Dean's case, they were signed by members of a full crew.

▶ Pam Reckelhoff holds a photo of her Uncle Earl above the ball turret, the position of the airplane in which he served.

CHARLES E. LYNN

CHARLES E. LYNN was a ball turret gunner in the 381st Bomb Group, serving aboard a B-17 that was christened *Stage Door Canteen*. The airplane was named by Mary Churchill, the daughter of the British prime minister, along with actors Vivien Leigh and Laurence Olivier. Charles was able to fly again onboard our aircraft in 2013, when we took it to Dothan, Alabama.

▲ Stage Door Canteens were a series of nightclubs where service men and women could spend an evening dancing and enjoying food and nonalcoholic drinks, with no cover charge. The popular establishments inspired a film of the same name in 1943, and, the following year, a B-17 followed suit. The airplane, part of the 381st Bomb Group, was christened after the name had been chosen by Mary Churchill (daughter of the British prime minister), seen standing near the microphone.

HOWARD BOBB

HOWARD BOBB served in the "Bloody 100th" Bomb Group, 349th Squadron, as a ball turret gunner, and was shot down twice. By the time the war was over, he had accumulated multiple confirmed kills. When our B-17 visited Cincinnati in 2013, his daughter, Pamela Bobb Byrd, came out to fly with us.

▲ Howard Bobb (leaning on the roof of the jeep) and some of his crew together near one of their B-17s after a mission.

JOHN TARABULA

JOHN TARABULA was a B-17 ball turret gunner in the 457th Bomb Group, 749th Bomb Squadron. He was also a planner. He had been dating a girl whom he nicknamed "Jo." Before leaving for combat he asked Jo's father for permission to marry her if he made it home. He received the green light and purchased a ring. He then placed the ring in a safety deposit box and gave her father the key and information on where it was. After completing his missions and getting word he was heading home, he wrote to his girlfriend.

▲ John Tarabula (front row, right) and members of his crew in their barracks.

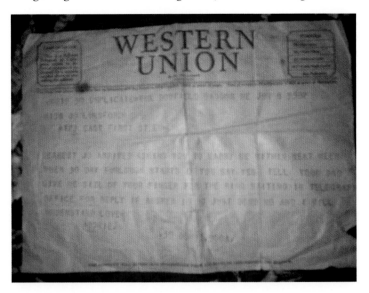

▲ That fateful Western Union telegram that John sent to his girl back home, asking for her hand in marriage.

He sent a Western Union telegram asking her to marry him. If she said yes, she was to let her father know, and he would take her down to get her ring.

Just as planned, she said yes, and they were celebrating their 69th wedding anniversary right about the time our aircraft was going to be in Lawrenceville, Georgia. We invited them to fly with us, and they accepted. They decided to bring their family along, too. I informed my co-workers, and they all pitched in for a cake to celebrate the Tarabulas' anniversary. Other departments at EAA also chipped in, and we provided a B-17 jacket for John and some B-17 earrings for Jo. When the time came we surprised them with everything and really made it a special day for them.

As they walked out to the B-17 to fly, John helped Jo onto the aircraft and then stopped short. "Oh, I am not getting in that thing," he said. A great laugh broke out, and then he further explained. "On my last mission our aircraft was damaged, and we were going to have to crash-land. I remember sitting in the back of the plane and asked God to get me out of this one and I will never fly again. Well, he did so now I have to live up to my end of the bargain." From the time of that last mission, John had never again flown in an airplane, and that was not about to change that day. Therefore, we took his daughter and wife up, and John went back for more cake.

▲ Jo and John cut their anniversary cake with their daughter, Cindy Tarabula Post.

CARL HARTMAN

CARL HARTMAN was another of the brave few who served as a ball turret gunner, in his case, aboard a B-17 assigned to the 490th Bomb Group named *Shoot You're Faded*.

We flew Carl's daughter, Lynne Newcomer, with us in 2014 at the Capital City Airport in Harrisburg, Pennsylvania.

"It took me back up through the ages, and I felt like I was right there with my father," she said. "To me he was the bravest man on Earth, and even flying in that plane I knew that that sunny day when we flew we weren't up high enough to be freezing cold like they were, with flak flying all around us, praying for our lives, and in fact there wasn't enough time to think about much at all, just get them all and head towards freedom and home!"

Lynne enjoyed it so much that she came back that weekend and flew again.

"The second time I went I got to help pull the props through. That was a cool experience," she said. "I always look at *Aluminum Overcast* as my plane!"

FRED ZURBUCHEN

FRED ZURBUCHEN was born and raised in Waupun, Wisconsin. He lied about his age to join the Army Air Forces and became a ball turret gunner on a B-17. On his 10th mission, a German 55 mm round exploded just outside of his turret. As he clambered out of the damaged turret, someone noticed he was bleeding. He also noticed limited movement of his knee. His crew discovered a piece of shrapnel from the flak had pierced his turret and struck him in the knee.

"I remember being able to see the white cliffs of Dover as we approached the field," he said. "We were able to land first as planes with wounded aboard were given priority. As we landed the ambulances rolled up and took me to the hospital where the doctor said that I may lose my leg. I said, the hell I will!"

Fred was supposed to be hospitalized for a few weeks to allow himself time to heal. He discovered just a few days after his ordeal that his crew was being sent on another mission with a replacement gunner. Rather than sit in a hospital, Fred climbed back into his turret with his crew.

"I couldn't stand the thought of them going without me," Fred said. He was just 17 years old. When people talk about the title of the greatest generation for our World War II veterans, I have always felt that Fred is a shining example of why they received the nickname.

Because Fred left the hospital, along with a records foul-up, he never received the Purple Heart he earned. His crew signed statements that he should have received it, but the record was never corrected. And he was too humble of a man to call attention to it as he never considered himself a hero. His grandkids made us aware of the oversight. Working with the U.S. Army, we were able to correct this. In our museum's Eagle Hangar, in front of his family, and with his wife, Betty, at his side, Fred received his medal. It was a medal long overdue, and one I am proud to say I played a small part in getting for him.

While Fred was off fighting the war, at home his girlfriend, Betty, was keeping busy. She worked full time and tried to help the war effort in any way she could, including growing a victory garden at her house. Victory gardens were grown not only in the country but also in urban areas. The thought behind it was that by growing your own vegetables and fruits, Americans could save canned goods — and the associated costs of labor and transportation — for the war effort.

"It made you feel like part of the war effort, that you were in this with them," Betty said. The U.S. Department of Agriculture estimated that more than 20 million victory gardens were planted and that they harvested 10 million tons of produce. Gardens were not the only thing Betty did on the homefront. She wrote letters to Fred to keep his spirits up. While on the surface the letters were about what was going on back home and everyday items, they held a far deeper meaning. To Fred, they were gold.

▲ The crew photo that flew with us in Minnesota in Fred's memory.

◀ Fred Zurbuchen holds his Purple Heart just moments after the surprise award.

TIMELESS VOICES

"I received a letter for every day that I was gone. Think about that," he said. "Here is Betty busy with work and everything else, and yet she managed to make sure she wrote me every day. And I never missed a day. Those letters meant the world to me. They meant the world to anyone getting a letter. Sometimes a friend would not hear from home for a while, and I always felt bad for them. I had this terrific girl back home that always made sure I knew I was being thought of."

Betty also had another special meaning, not just to Fred, but to the whole crew. She was painted on the nose of their B-17. I had the chance to ask Betty how she felt about her likeness being painted on the nose.

"I think it was great. I flew every mission with him," she said. When Fred returned home, it was Betty who picked him up at the train station in Beaver Dam, Wisconsin. I am extremely fortunate to call Fred, Betty, and their family my friends, and have always said that Fred and Betty are American treasures.

On the weekend of July 4, 2019, I went on tour to Minnesota with our B-17 and B-25. While we were preparing for the first flight of the day on Friday, I received word that Fred died in his sleep, passing peacefully next to his bride. It was an emotional day. I had lost veterans whom we had flown before. However, Fred was my friend. We printed a copy of one of Fred's wartime photos, taped it into the ball turret, and that weekend Fred flew with us one last time. I went to his funeral and delivered the photo along with a note about it flying with us to his family. I felt that it was our special way of paying tribute to a great man. While on the surface it may not be much, I like to think Fred would approve of the honor we gave him.

DOUG WARD

I FIRST MET Doug Ward in the summer of 2013. Being a new employee, but also interested in the B-17 program, I was assigned to the EAA Welcome Center near the main plaza during EAA AirVenture Oshkosh. My supervisor told me Doug was to be my partner, and the two of us would be working together to sell rides in our B-17. I looked over our workstation, wanting to make sure he would be comfortable if he was using a walker, or even a wheelchair. After a few moments, I heard a yell from outside the tent.

"Hey, Chrissy Boy!" There sat my partner, not in a wheelchair or walker, but atop a 10-speed bicycle. I remember thinking to myself that he couldn't possibly be a WWII veteran, as he looked like he was in his 60s. But he was indeed a veteran. He flew 25 missions in the ball turret of a B-17 in the 305th Bomb Group based at RAF Chelveston. For that week, I got to hang out with a B-17 veteran and hear stories of what his life was like, details about his missions, and the living conditions at his base. He once told me about the time his friend was in the ball turret of a B-17 next to him in formation and took a flak hit.

TIMELESS VOICES

"When we landed back at Chelveston, I ran from my airplane over to where they had parked his," he said. "I wanted to see if my friend was all right. I got to his aircraft in time to see the fire crews there. They were hosing his remains out of the turret. That is all that was left of my friend."

He kept me spellbound with his stories. And it wasn't just me. Visitors with an interest in history would come to see him. Some folks made the journey to the Welcome Center for no other reason than to see Doug. And it wasn't just older history nuts, either — young people flocked to Doug to hear his stories as well.

▲ Doug Ward looking over his turret just prior to a mission.

◄ Top, a young Doug Ward climbing into his ball turret in Chelveston, England during WWII. Bottom, Doug does it again, some 70 years later. "I think I can still get back in the ball," he told me, and he was right.

▲ Edgar L. Harrell served as a ball turret gunner on the B-17 *Times A Wastin*, and was killed in action in April 1945. Years later, this would spark his grandson, Gary Hall, to continue to work on preserving the memories of these brave men.

▲ Another ball turret gunner, Sgt. Donald Herman, smiles as he shows off the cramped quarters of his crew station.

Over the next few years Doug and his wonderful girlfriend, Judie Ohm, shared with us the joy that is the EAA fly-in convention. Doug also came to support the many events our museum had throughout the years. He always had a smile on his face and time to talk. Doug died January 26, 2018, at age 94. I knew when I met him I was in for an adventure, and I was right. The time I spent with him I will always cherish, and never forget.

WAIST GUNS

THE B-17'S WAIST GUNNER stations are situated in the rear fuselage, aft of the ball turret, and consist of a window on each side, each equipped with a single .50-caliber machine gun. Early variants used a glass bubble or blister in this area, but those were replaced by simple windows to reduce drag. On E and F models, the gunners would fire through an open window with frigid air blowing right into the fuselage. Wind deflectors were mounted on each side, but the guys said they really didn't do much to keep the wind and cold out. Later G models had an enclosed glass window with the gun firing through it. Waist gunners stood back to back for hours patrolling the skies for aircraft waiting to get a kill.

OSCAR W. KRIGBAUM

TECH SGT. OSCAR W. KRIGBAUM was a waist gunner in the 306th Bomb Group, 368th Bomb Squadron. During a mission in the spring of 1943 he was wounded by flak. Despite his wounds, he crawled back to his gun in the waist section of his B-17 and continued to fire at fighters. He can be seen getting a blood transfusion in the famous William Wyler documentary *Memphis Belle*. He was later awarded the Silver Star Medal for his actions that day. He also met the king and queen of the United Kingdom and spoke on BBC Radio. His son flew with us in Waterloo, Iowa.

◄ Oscar Krigbaum and the crew of the B-17 *Eager Beaver* of the 306th Bomb Group.

ROY O'NEIL

I FIRST CONNECTED with Roy O'Neil in a surprising way, while I was working on a B-17 that was painted to honor a wartime airplane named *Miss Liberty Belle*. I had started a thread about the airplane in the popular Warbird Information Xchange online forum and was stunned to see that Roy had replied! Roy was a waist gunner in the 305th Bomb Group based at RAF Chelveston. On several occasions he flew missions on the original B-17, *Miss Liberty Belle*. Roy flew his last combat mission on November 26, 1944, and when the crew returned, the aircraft had 30 holes in it, including one that was just a couple of feet from Roy's head.

▲ Members of the 305th Bomb Group pose with the Nazi flag presented to them in a publicity photo.

He did a phone interview with me, and in one conversation he told me about the famous 305th flag. During the first big missions to Schweinfurt, the 305th took heavy losses. In April 1945, the 42nd Infantry Division captured the city of Schweinfurt and sent a recovered Nazi flag to the 8th Air Force. The flag made its way to the men of the 305th Bomb Group, where a few publicity photos were taken. Then, after the photos were taken the men took the flag behind a Nissen hut, threw it in the mud, and urinated on it.

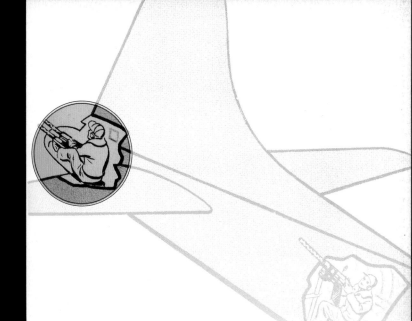

TAIL GUNS

LAST BUT CERTAINLY NOT least on the flight crew was the tail gunner. He sat, isolated from the crew, in the absolute rear of the aircraft, on a bicycle seat, facing backward. He fired his twin .50-caliber guns at any enemy that approached from the rear of the Flying Fortress, and kept the pilot informed about any threats from behind.

JACK DEMPSEY ROBERTSON

JACK DEMPSEY ROBERTSON was one of those who was so upset by the attack on Pearl Harbor that he knew he had to do something. He lied about his age to join the U.S. Army Air Forces on December 8, 1941, and became a B-17 tail gunner. His airplane was so shot up that on three different occasions the crew returned to base on foot. He flew 99 missions and received the Purple Heart twice. Jack's niece and her husband came out to see our airplane in June of 2013.

CALVIN G. TURKINGTON

STAFF SGT. CALVIN G. TURKINGTON was a B-17 tail gunner in the 303rd Bomb Group, and he flew 35 missions. On September 28, 1944, on a mission to Magdeburg, Germany, in B-17 *Miss Umbriago* he was severely wounded. He managed to crawl to the waist compartment, where he died. The plane crashed near Wittmar, Germany. Calvin's body was found in the crashed B-17 and was later interred at the Netherlands American Cemetery at Margraten, Netherlands. Calvin's daughter, Nancy Kapp, flew with us in Salem, Oregon.

▲ Calvin (fourth from left, front row) and his crew pose with their base's pet dog.

JACK DODSON

JACK DODSON SHARED some time on the phone with me on a cold January day in 2016. He served in the 398th Bomb Group and flew 35 missions in the tail. He said the coldest he remembers it was close to 60 below zero.

"Of course you didn't notice the cold so much when the flak started coming up," he said. The cold he described along with the cold here in snowy Wisconsin really helped set the tone for his stories.

JACK WALLACE

JACK WALLACE was a California boy assigned as a tail gunner in the 91st Bomb Group. His B-17 was named *Shirley Jean* and, like so many others, was adorned with a pinup girl on the nose. He flew with us in Ukiah, California. I asked if he could sum up what a mission was like in one word, what that word would be. He said, "Cold."

On his first few missions he tried to take fruit like oranges up to have as a snack. After all, these missions lasted sometimes up to eight hours or more.

"It would have been great, but everything kept freezing," he said. "So I had to fall back to plan B. I would take Snickers bars up

▲ Jack Wallace (kneeling, front row, second from left) and his crew with the B-17, *Shirley Jean*, of the 91st Bomb Group.

▲ Jack onboard our B-17 decades later, reflecting on the day and his past.

▲ Jack with the tail guns of our B-17 during a California visit.

with me." From that day forward, he always had Snickers bars in his home. His daughter called the day after his flight and said that during their previous visit he was not feeling too well. But the day of his flight, when they went to pick him up, he seemed like his old vibrant self again. Being around a B-17 has that effect on people, acting at times as a four-engine fountain of youth for World War II veterans. Jack and his daughter, Vikki, went out to the aircraft, and a flood of memories both good and bad came back to Jack due to an extra surprise we had planned for him. As he climbed in, a wartime photo of his crew and him in front of *Shirley Jean* greeted him. The photo was taped to the rear bulkhead. After that day, Jack and I kept in touch, and I'd call and ask him questions. Then one day I got word from his daughter that he had died. The world was short one hero that day. As a little tribute to him, our crew had Snickers bars passed out near the aircraft with a little description as to the why.

When we informed Vikki, she was touched but didn't understand the candy bar part of it. I explained the story he'd told me.

"Well that makes a lot of sense now," she said. "He always had that candy at his house, and we just figured he liked them." Vikki later flew with us as well and got to share the experience of what it was like up in a B-17.

▲ Sgt. Harry "Red" Oestreich (second from left) of the 95th Bomb Group and his crew. When we placed the call out looking for veterans to join us, he was always willing to come and represent the tail gunners.

◄ A 91st Bomb Group B-17, named *Miss Minookie*, of the 323rd Bomb Squadron. The tail gunner for this aircraft was Staff Sgt. Willard P. Chandler whose son, Doug Chandler, is active in keeping the memory alive for these heroes.

GROUND CREW

THE DAY BEGAN and ended with the ground crew. This dedicated group of men did everything they could to keep their B-17 in the best operating condition possible. Even though they were not flying the missions, they still certainly fought the war. Everything they did on the ground had to stand up to the rigors of combat 5 miles up. The repairs they made and the maintenance they performed on the big bombers were the difference between life and death up there. Maintaining this fleet of aircraft routinely required the crews to stay up all night repairing combat damage to get as many aircraft as possible ready for the next mission. On many occasions they were forced to work out in the elements. When they were done they watched the bombers take off and fly out of sight, and when word came that they were almost home, they went out and waited to see if their aircraft had returned, an exercise that was known as "sweating out the mission." Many of the guys moved their tents to the hard stands where the airplanes parked in an effort to stay even closer to their work.

BOB MORELLI

BOB MORELLI grew up in Beaver Falls, Pennsylvania. When the war broke out he tried to join the Navy but couldn't pass the physical. He graduated from high school when he was just 16 and then attended the Pittsburgh Institute of Aeronautics, where he earned his airframe and powerplant certificates. He was drafted into the U.S. Army Air Forces in 1944, just two months after his 18th birthday. After a two-week voyage to Europe aboard a Liberty ship, Bob was assigned to the 306th Bomb Group stationed at RAF Thurleigh. There he repaired components for the B-17s.

"I did a lot of work in the shops. We did a lot of fabric and sheet metal repairs," Bob said. He described the noise at the base as deafening.

"In the daytime, the American bombers would be taxiing and taking off," he said. "Then at night while we would be winding down, it would start all over again. This time, it was the RAF bombers going out." Bob spent his downtime with guys having a few beers and of course writing letters home to his mother. While doing their work, the ground crews always knew what was on the line.

"You always double-checked your work. We knew that the crews depended on the work we were doing," he said.

After about six months Bob was transferred to a base in France to help maintain aircraft taking part in mapping sorties that were known as the Casey Jones missions.

"When the war ended I was sent home on a ship," he said. "It took us longer to get home because our ship broke for about four days." When Bob arrived home in Beaver Falls he couldn't wait to catch up on local events and news.

"In the days at the end of the war, it was great when you'd find out a friend was home," he said. "We'd have a homecoming, and all of the guys I hung around came back here."

It's important to me that Bob Morelli's story is told here. Like many of our veterans he is a humble hero, proud of his service and his part in the war effort, but quiet about it. Bob is also one of the people who helped pave the way for me to get involved in aviation. He took a chance on a 12-year-old kid who wanted to volunteer at a museum way back when, and now he and his family are like family to me. I wouldn't get to do what I do now without his help.

▲ When Bob was just a kid, he worked on Stinsons for All American Airways as they delivered the mail. This photo was taken on one of the many trips to Oshkosh we have enjoyed together.

▲ Our B-17 is a living, breathing machine. As such, out on the road it requires the skillful work of the mechanics who travel along with it. Our crew is top notch!

◄ Mechanics worked tirelessly to ensure that their airplanes were always in good working order.

THE HOMEFRONT

WHEN THE WAR CAME to the United States, the nation responded with a sense of purpose — and the military power to back it up — the likes of which had never been seen before. From rationing programs and victory gardens to vital jobs on the homefront as well as the frontlines, everyone did their part to help the war effort in their own way.

◀ Another photo saved by Don England, this one of a B-17 wing nearing completion. At the height of production, 16 B-17s were produced per day in Seattle.

ROSIE

A GERMAN TANK COMMANDER was once overheard saying, "The German Tiger tank was as good as 10 of your American Shermans. The problem was you Americans always had 11." The United States produced an arsenal like no one had ever seen before and much of it was built by women. Most men were dedicated to serving in the military, which left large holes in the workforce. Between 1940 and 1945, the female percentage of the U.S. workforce increased from 27 percent to nearly 37 percent, and by 1945 nearly one out of every four married women worked outside the home. In total, about 310,000 women took production jobs during World War II, with the aviation industry seeing the largest increase in female workers. Prior to the war just 1 percent of the aviation industry's workforce was women. By 1945 that had grown to 65 percent. Another 350,000 women served in the armed forces. The name "Rosie the Riveter" stems from an image painted by Norman Rockwell for the cover of the May 29, 1943, issue of the *Saturday Evening Post*. Eventually, it became synonymous with all of the women working in the production force.

JUNE MORRIS

JUNE "SMOKEY" MORRIS is a fantastic example of a Rosie. She riveted on the night shift during WWII at Boeing in Seattle. She installed the auxiliary fuel tanks on each B-17 that left Boeing for the United Kingdom. Hers was the last task on the line before the bomber flew out the next day for its base in the combat theater. One day Smokey heard over the radio that a German wolf pack had sunk a freighter in the Caribbean on which her father served as an engineer. Smokey reported to her night shift at Boeing anyway. That happened to be the night the union went on strike. When the union rep told her she had to go on strike, Smokey said no. She told him that the Germans had just killed her daddy, and she was going to personally make sure that this bird was ready to go after Germans tomorrow morning. The union rep could not persuade her to strike, and finally he told her that he would drag her out of the hangar if he had to. She invited him to come up onto the wing and get her. Her bucker, Helen, echoed the same challenge, and the union rep backed off and left.

The giant hangar was empty except for those two women riveting through the night. Their supervisor, not daring to argue with them, reluctantly stayed and kept the lights on. The next day, that bomber lifted off for the United Kingdom. June had just turned 90 when our B-17 was visiting Seattle on its tour. June had built thousands of B-17s but had never flown in one. I am proud to say on that sunny day in Seattle we changed that for her. She emerged from the aircraft with a smile and then took the reporters who were there covering the event over to the lower wing area and gave them a thorough dissertation on rivets.

CATHERINE JONES

AS PREVIOUSLY MENTIONED, due to the demand on Boeing to produce B-17s along with its other aircraft like the highly advanced B-29 Superfortress, other companies were enlisted to help build B-17s. This ensured that enough of the type were produced and delivered to the combat forces. In addition to Boeing, Douglas Aircraft and Lockheed Vega also produced the B-17. *Aluminum Overcast* is actually one of the more than 2,000 built by Lockheed Vega. Catherine's flight was a special one for all of us. She was a Rosie who worked on the B-17 line at Lockheed. She mentioned that early on she helped repair airplanes that had been rotated back after combat damage.

"There were times I'd be working in the waist section and come across blood still in there," she said. Catherine was working on the assembly line when *Aluminum Overcast* was built, so there is an excellent chance that some of those rivets are hers She helped us wrap up the 2015 tour as she took a flight in "her" B-17 on November 22 of that year.

BETTY LAUSCH

WHEN BETTY'S HUSBAND, Bryson Lausch, was called to war, she did not just sit at home and wait for his return. She took a job in a production plant, driving rivets on B-17s in Seattle. Meanwhile, Bryson served as a tail gunner in the 97th Bomb Group. She always thought that maybe the work she was doing would somehow get to him, and he would fly in a B-17 that she built. Due to the nature of how Boeing assembled its aircraft in sections, she had never seen a B-17 together in one piece. That all changed in 2017 when she flew with us in Olympia, Washington.

◀ Betty Lausch and volunteer Marie Samson, who was working a tour stop and dressed the part of Rosie.

WASP

MORE THAN 350,000 WOMEN signed up to serve in the U.S. armed forces during World War II, including the first women to fly military aircraft in this country. They were known as the Women Airforce Service Pilots, or WASP. They would serve mainly as ferry pilots as the factories were producing aircraft faster than they could be delivered — and when they were delivered, it meant tying up male pilots who would otherwise be assigned to combat units overseas. The legendary Jackie Cochran was among those who fought to get women the right to fly these machines. These women were also required to learn to fly most of this county's arsenal of aircraft, so one WASP knew how to fly many aircraft, not just one type.

◀ WASP members Frances Green, Margaret "Peg" Kirchner, Ann Waldner, and Blanche Osborn deliver another B-17 to Lockbourne Army Air Base in Ohio.

BETTY STROHFUS

I AM NOT SURE how to start talking about Betty. Betty was born into a large family of six kids in 1919 in Minnesota. She borrowed $100 from the bank to start her flying career as she joined an all-male aviators club. When the war broke out, she saw an opportunity to help. She joined the newly formed WASP and became one of just 1,074 women who flew the U.S. fleet of powerful fighters, bombers, transports, and trainers. And she flew them all, including the B-17. Her favorite was the T-6 Texan.

"I used to love landing, and then pulling up to the gas pumps. I would get out and take my flying gear off, and all of my hair would fall down to my shoulders," she said. "It was fun to watch the reactions of the guys working the fuel stations when they found out that a woman was flying this thing." We spent a special day with her in our museum in Oshkosh where we had her name placed on the T-6 in our collection. We walked her up to it without her knowing and gave her a pretty good surprise. Months later when the B-17 was in Minnesota, she flew in the Flying Fortress again. Betty was just a firecracker. At the age of 71 she became one of the first women to fly an F-16, and at the age of 95 she flew in an aerobatic aircraft. Betty died in 2016 at the age of 96.

▶ The black-and-white photo is of Betty Strohfus with a BT-13 while she was flying at Avenger Field. The inset photo is of her and a WWII B-25 pilot on a tour stop in Minnesota when she went flying with us.

THEY EARNED THEIR WINGS

We proudly honor the dedicated women who served as WASP, flying them aboard our B-17 whenever possible, paying tribute to them as we would any other veteran.

RED CROSS

THEY WERE KNOWN AS the "Doughnut Dollies," young women in their 20s and 30s, all volunteers, who would drive a special vehicle to deliver hot, fresh doughnuts, something to drink, and most of all a momentary escape from the war.

◄ Red Cross worker resting in a jeep with some of the ground crew at Chelveston, England.

BLANCHE (BARNES) GANGWERE

KANSAS CITY NATIVE Blanche Barnes was just briefly married when she had to send her husband, Lt. Leslie Barnes, a B-24 bombardier, off to war in North Africa. Not long after she received the telegram no one wanted: Her husband had been killed in action. While grieving her loss, she decided to do something to help the war effort. She was inspired by a newsreel about the Clubmobile girls of the Red Cross. The Clubmobile was a truck driven around to various bases to hand out food and other items to make the troops feel a little closer to home.

"They sure were always excited to see an American girl," Blanche said. "We would dance to some of the records which we would keep on board." Many times Blanche would hand out doughnuts to the crews waiting to board their aircraft and take off. Many of those crews would never return.

"It's something that still makes me cry today when I think about it," she said. "You would get to know a young man, then he would go fly a mission. As they returned home, sometimes the bombers would crash and many often would never make it home. It has always stayed with me."

When she flew with us in June 2013, we wanted to do something special for her. One of our B-17 crew members, Lisa Toll, and I decided to buy some boxes of doughnuts and have them decorated with copies of her wartime photos. She was shocked by something as small as that recognition for what she did for the

▲ Blanche handing out doughnuts to the crews of the 303rd Bomb Group.

war effort. But it's nothing compared to the moments she shared with air crew members that provided relief and comfort in a time of conflict.

THOSE WHO FLY HER TODAY

Sean Elliott is not just one of our B-17 pilots — he is the check airman for EAA's air operations department as well as the vice president of advocacy and safety. Sean works in the area he does largely due to the influence he had from a member of America's greatest generation.

"Growing up, my grandfather, Lt. Francis Edward Rudhman, very much played the role of my father," Sean said. "He had been a naval aviator in the Second World War. He flew a large number of aircraft at Naval Air Station Glenview, and then served flying the Navy version of the C-47 known as the R4D in the Naval Air Transport Command in VR-3, and finally VR-11. He was very open with me about talking about the flights he had been on, and I could not get enough."

His grandfather recalled a special mission where he flew Adm. William Halsey around Leyte Gulf.

"I remember listening to him and just thinking that we will never fully understand what they went through," he said. "Flying some of these vintage aircraft takes all of your situational awareness. To then think that they were flying under combat conditions, with people shooting at them ... is truly amazing."

Sean also pointed out the age at which we were placing such high demands.

"I am a pilot with over 9,000 hours, and I couldn't imagine the people doing it in their teens and 20s with something like 300 to 400 hours," he said. Through Sean's college years and the start of his aviation career, he never lost the excitement and passion instilled in him by his grandfather.

"I always enjoyed two aspects the most. Teaching and watching someone who maybe had to work harder to get proficient finally have the lightbulb come on and start really growing," he said. "The other was my continued love of vintage aircraft. It was a great opportunity to come to EAA to combine both of my passions."

It takes a different kind of pilot to fly the vintage World War II aircraft. Sean noted that people have to come at it from a different perspective.

"The type of flying that is required in these older aircraft requires a skill that is not generally taught anymore," he said. "You have to be a stick and rudder pilot as opposed to a systems manager, which a lot of the modern aircraft train you to be. You have to climb into something like the B-17 with a completely different level of respect."

For Sean, the climb to the B-17 cockpit began in EAA's 1929 Ford Tri-Motor.

"When I started flying the Ford I was flying it off Pioneer Airport," he said. "That is the grass runway right behind the EAA museum. That is not a long runway for the Ford, and there are a lot of strange winds that blow through there." Sean would soon find himself in a seat very special to him, the pilot seat of a DC-3, the civilian version of the aircraft his grandfather had flown in the Navy.

"The DC-3 was very special to me. I thought about him every time I sat in that seat. He always loved the DC-3 but said that the ultimate achievement for a pilot was to fly a four-engine aircraft," he said. That was Sean's next stop as he started training in the B-17.

▲ Sean Elliott has flown the aircraft on many special occasions and ensures that our operation is safe and impactful.

"I started on the B-17 in 2001 in the co-pilot side of things and then moved to the left seat as an aircraft commander in 2004 when I got checked out," he said. "My first impression was, 'Wow, this is a lot of airplane.' I had great preparation work here, so I was not overwhelmed, but the aircraft was a challenge." Many of the challenges that Sean and our team face occur on the tour that the aircraft flies all around the country.

"Out on tour everything changes. Amounts of people, winds, runways and taxiways, density altitudes, strange gusts that occur at certain airports," he said. "All of this is a part of the experience. You have to always be thinking ahead of the airplane. From the approach to the turns in the taxiways ahead. Your head has to be in the game from the time you strap into the cockpit until the time you put the chocks back in."

Sean has had many special flights on the B-17, but a few stand out.

"One of the most memorable flights for me was when we took EAA founder Paul Poberezny up for his last flight in it," he said. "I had flown with him a lot, and I was always amazed by his skill. At any time he could just get in it and fly it with the same level of confidence as he always had."

Another flight that stands out for Sean is when the B-17 took part in the graduation ceremony for a class of test pilots at Edwards Air Force Base in California. The new pilots had the chance to fly with Sean and our crew in the B-17.

"We had B-52 pilots and fighter pilots, but I remember one pilot in particular who had flown low-level missions in the B-1 bomber," he said. "Here he was wrestling the B-17 around. When we landed, he was covered with sweat and just looked at me and said in relief, 'Man, this is a lot of airplane.' It was rewarding to see pilots who had flown powerful jet aircraft on combat missions still humbled by the B-17."

In May 2015 our B-17 took part in a ceremony to commemorate the 70th anniversary of Victory in Europe Day. On that day several types of World War II aircraft were assembled near Washington, D.C., and then flown over the National Mall. Sean and our B-17 led the B-17 element in the flyover.

"It was amazing to watch all of the familiar monuments and the Capitol building go by under the airplane," he said.

When asked if there is one story from his time flying the B-17 that stands out over the others, he said he always goes back to one woman.

"She was not a veteran; she actually flew with us on the media flight in Lakeland, Florida," he said. "We had landed and shut down, and about everyone had already climbed out of the aircraft. There was one woman left sitting back by the waist guns just crying. I stopped and asked her if she was okay. She explained to me that her father had been a waist gunner on a B-17 in the war. He was killed in May of 1943. She was born in April of the same year. She always wanted to know more about her father, and what his experience was like. Now after this flight, she had an idea of what his life was like onboard a B-17."

▶ Our *Aluminum Overcast* showing off the wonderful lines Boeing put together, as well as the bold colors of the 398th Bomb Group.

Pilot: Bob Abresch, 398th Bomb Group; Co-Pilot: Scott Welch, 397th Bomb Group; Bombardier: William R. Meier, 96th Bomb Group; Bombardier: Robert F. Schneider, 351st Bomb Group;

Navigator: Bill Bergner, 92nd Bomb Group; Top Turret Gunner/Flight Engineer: Chet E. Gardeski, 305th Bomb Group; Radio Operator: Harvin Abrahamson, 487th Bomb Group;

Ball Turret Gunner: Fred Zurbuchen, 493rd Bomb Group; Waist Gunner: Bob Schuh, 398th Bomb Group; Tail Gunner: Harry Oestreich, 95th Bomb Group

FREEDOM FLIGHT

APRIL 14, 2014

My friends and I were gathered one night, and as is often the case, the conversation turned to aircraft and the crews who flew in World War II. One of my friends mentioned that it would probably be impossible to reunite a full 10-man B-17 crew due to the dwindling numbers of our veterans from that era. After doing some research I quickly found out he was correct. We could not find a full crew or anywhere near it, even after talking to many relevant veterans groups. So we decided to assemble our own crew — 10 veterans who had flown or served aboard the airplane in combat and could come together one more time to represent their old crew station.

I worked with the museum curator who also managed EAA's oral history program, Timeless Voices of Aviation. Through past interviews he had done along with a few volunteers he knew of, we were able to find about half of our crew. Calling them at home was an experience in itself. My script was the same for them all.

I would call, and an older-sounding voice would answer the phone.

I would start with, "Hello, my name is Chris, and I am with EAA in Oshkosh."

The older voice would usually respond "Okay" a bit cautiously, in case this was a sales call.

Then I would continue, "Is this the gentleman who was a top turret gunner on B-17s?"

I would get a cautious, "Yes, it is."

Then I laid out our plan. "We have a B-17 here, and we are putting a crew back together." After that, my friends nicknamed me "Elwood" in a nod to *The Blues Brothers* and their efforts to get the band back together. The response I would get this time from the veteran was different. It was warmer, and you could almost hear his youth snap right back.

Their responses ranged from "I'm in" to "Where are we going?" I also worked with the 8th Air Force Historical Society, and together we got our 10 veterans, from bombardier to tail gunner and everyone in between. It was no easy task. It took about three months of phone calls and emails. Several times, we had all 10 crew members and then one became not well enough to go. One man died, further driving home the importance of this flight.

We had a great day planned. The veterans would arrive at our museum in the morning in mid-April. We would have WWII-era Army jeeps and trucks, courtesy of our friends at the Military Veterans Museum in Oshkosh, lined up in front of the museum. After spending a little time together the veterans would load into the trucks and be driven to the B-17 with a full police escort.

▲ Sean Elliott and the modern crew of our B-17 meet the wartime crew of a B-17.

▲ Members of the Freedom Flight crew enjoy their time together as the U.S. Army presents awards created by Doug Chandler. Once they got near one another, they turned into 20-year-olds all over again. From left to right are Fred Zurbuchen, Harvin Abrahamson, and Bob Schneider.

The night before our special mission I did not sleep at all. I was thinking through all of the details, and hoping for good weather. In the early morning hours snow began to fall and coated the ground. It was only a few inches, but I was worried that it might be enough to keep the military vehicles away. A warm bus was our alternate option. Then the time came for the guys to arrive. One of the details that really made the day special was that their families were invited to come along and witness the day. For the families it was a chance for some of them to see their fathers and grandfathers in a light in which they have never seen them before. We were wondering if all 10 would make it that morning. One by one they arrived at the museum. Watching them interact with one another was educational in itself. They would introduce themselves to one another followed by phrases like, 'I'm your tail gunner." All I could think of while watching this was that this is how they must have come together as a crew back in the 1940s.

The time came for them to ride over to see the airplane. As we walked outside I was shocked to see the vintage military vehicles from the Military Veterans Museum. They had braved the snow and cold, and arrived in time to transport these warriors. I mentioned that it was very cold, around 30 degrees Fahrenheit, and that maybe it would be better to ride in the warm bus. One of the vets passed by me, gave me a smile, and said, "Don't worry, it wasn't always warm in England either." He then turned back and climbed into the vintage jeep waiting for him. The families either rode in the warm bus or piled into one of the army trucks.

As we started to pull away, I noticed that the EAA staff had lined the road, some with flags and signs, to cheer on the veterans. As we drove over to Kermit Weeks Hangar where the B-17 was kept, the police had the intersections blocked, and each officer was standing at attention saluting the veterans as they went by. When we arrived at the hangar, it was like going back in time. To see these veterans walk up to their old aircraft was a priceless moment. While some of them had canes and walkers, the moment they arrived near the aircraft they seemed to not need them as much or even at all in some cases. They stood at the nose for a crew photo. Bob Abresch very abruptly and without prior conversation exclaimed, "Ten-hut!" which was the order to stand at attention. All 10 men quickly snapped to attention and saluted. It was an extremely patriotic moment.

The crew members were shocked when they saw we had their names on the aircraft below their crew stations. It was incredibly emotional to watch the families interact with their loved ones. Each veteran right away went to his old station and started showing folks what it was that he did. One of my most cherished memories of the day was watching our bombardier, Robert Schneider, sitting on the floor in his compartment with his teenage great-granddaughter, who was sitting in his old seat, as they ran over all of the equipment and what he did. We were not sure if the weather was going to clear enough for the flight, and the *Aluminum Overcast* crew was watching intently for any break in the weather. The best news of the day was when Sean Elliott came out and said, "Okay, we have a window to take them up. Let's get her out of the hangar."

One by one, the crew members climbed into their old mount to go up one more time. Families watched their fathers and grandfathers with a different feeling about them. A few of the families remarked that they watched the relative they have always known and loved transform into the hero that was never talked about. Friends, family, media, and supporters all stood by, waiting to see them airborne, to see a 10-man B-17 crew flying. To see once again a 10-man B-17 crew flying. I will never forget the sense of joy and patriotism that rushed over me as I watched that silver Fortress climb above the hangars and toward the heavens. I was overwhelmed at the thought of a B-17 flying with a full crew, a group of 10 humble heroes who stood in for thousands of their comrades, many of whom gave their lives decades ago to guarantee the freedoms we enjoy today. Every mission that *Aluminum Overcast* flies is special, but this one was truly unique. To this day, that flight is one of the best days of my life.

When the airplane taxied in, the fire department was there to spray a water cannon salute over the aircraft as it went by.

The airplane was pulled into the hangar, and one by one the crew climbed off, all with smiles and a few deep in reflection. One of them came over to thank me. He said, "Thank you for giving us back our airplane." I was surprised because he had flown on a B-17 a few years prior at an air show. I asked him what he meant. He said, "Yes, I flew on a B-17 a few years ago. But that was in July, and it was 80 degrees. Today up there, with the rest of my crew, we had our plane back. It was cold. We could see our breath as we were up there. That is what it was like." I still get chills thinking about his remarks.

This flight will always remain one of the events I am most proud of being a part of while here at EAA.

▲ B-17 co-pilot Scott Welch enjoying himself as EAA staff members welcome our veterans. Scott recalled a fellow crew member saving their lives. "He told me to move to the right, and I did," he said. "The next moment, an 88 mm shell exploded right where the plane had been. That would have taken the plane down for sure. I figured if one of my crew mates asked me to do something, I'd do it, then ask about it later on the ground."

▲ Fred Zurbuchen with his great grandchildren as he showed them where he worked during the war.

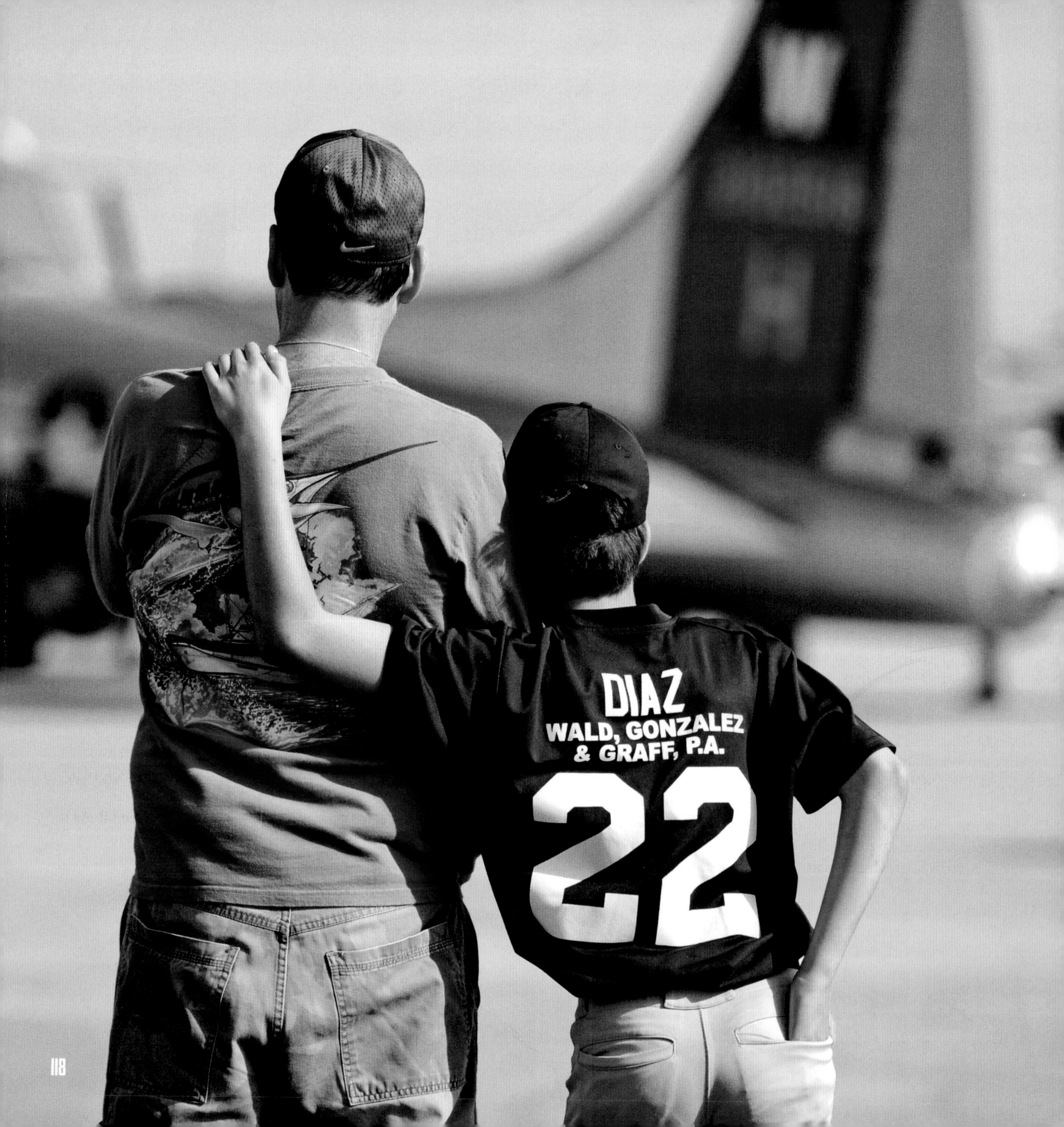
DIAZ
WALD, GONZALEZ
& GRAFF, P.A.
22

THE FAMILIES

One of the things I had hoped to accomplish with our B-17 Flight Experience program was to honor the crews who flew combat and the women who were stateside doing their part. I hoped to educate and inspire our youth by honoring these heroes. The one thing I was not prepared for was the friendships I gained through this aircraft. I found myself friends with so many of these amazing men and women from what we call the greatest generation. But the friendships did not stop there. The families of these amazing people also quickly became fast friends. What I find thrilling about the whole experience is watching sons and daughters who have known their father literally their whole life suddenly see him in a different way as he speaks of his mission in the airplane, his role in the war, and the buddies he flew with. Some of the stories were hilarious; others would send you reeling with heartache. All the while, I've felt such great pride in our country as well as in what these people did to preserve our way of life.

This is the true mission of our aircraft.

One of the hardest things I have had to deal with in this role is that I blindly become friends with these people who are larger than life. I fail to see age. So when I lose one of them, it hurts just as bad as if I have lost a friend my age. It hurts, but it is worth the pain. In the tail gunner section of the book I mentioned Vikki

Hild. Her father was Jack Wallace, a 91st Bomb Group B-17 tail gunner. If I was having a down day or something was bothering me, I called Jack and talked B-17s for a while. He was always happy to have the call. After his death, Vikki and I both still feel a void.

In November 2013, we were privileged to fly the B-17 over historic Lambeau Field, home of the Green Bay Packers football team. Our B-17 would perform the flyover to start the game. I called home and told my father to tune in to the game as our aircraft would be on TV. The NFL had every camera pointed on our aircraft, cameras were in the bomb bay, and a few friends and I were next to the stadium freezing while we anticipated the arrival of our aircraft. And I mean freezing. We watched as the airplane thundered overhead and made a beautiful approach to the stadium. Then we climbed into our warm cars and headed home. The next day we received a thank-you email. As it turns out, just blocks from the stadium, a family was laying to rest their loved one. He had served in the war and was a top turret gunner on B-17s in the 398th Bomb Group. They were just leaving the funeral home as our B-17 went sailing by. To them, it was a sight they will never forget. I think fate put us all together that day. We set off thinking we were going to do something cool, and little did we know we created an unforgettable memory for a family and hopefully helped in the healing process from a tough loss.

▲ The MacBeth family, who flew with their grandfather, a B-17 navigator during the war. They filled an entire airplane, and also brought his friend, who was a bombardier.

▶ The B-17 captures the imaginations of people of all ages, inspiring them to come out and visit, and hear stories of what family members before them had done.

I arranged a media flight for the family of a radio operator who was killed during the war. Only his dog tags returned. After the flight, they sent me a thank-you card along with something else in the envelope. In that envelope was one of his dog tags. The note thanked me and asked me to wear the tag, not just let it sit in a drawer somewhere. I cherish it to this day. Not a day goes by that I do not look at it and think of a man I'd never met, a man who sacrificed everything in defense of our country. I often reflect on what it must have meant to that family to fly in our airplane, and I am humbled that they trusted me with the honor of wearing that tag.

The most powerful one for me remains the family of a gunner we flew. We arranged for him and his family to fly on a preview flight with members of local media. It was going to be a great day for this vet as his small hometown news was there to cover him flying in his old airplane once more. What many forget is that the heroes from the war came not just from the big cities, but also from small towns many of us have never or will never hear of. When they achieved any success in the war, they made the town's headlines, and it was the same when they came home. Our media flights are a chance to have those veterans make the front page again, so that the town can also be proud of their contribution and their hero. The veteran's family had traveled to be there for his big day, some of them actually coming in from great distances.

Then that morning, a Hollywood celebrity stole the headlines by pulling some stunt that took all of the media's attention. The members of the media who were set to fly with us canceled to cover the breaking story from Hollywood. I was heartbroken. The easy thing for us to do would have been to cancel the flight. But that is not what our air tours manager, Kristy Busse, wanted. She felt we had made a promise to this veteran and to his family, and we were going to fly them. I was elated that our veteran was still going up. The flight crew at the aircraft filled the rest of the airplane with his family members, so the flight was even more special as he was going with his sons and grandkids. The next Monday I received a call from his son. We have a flight jacket that we sell that features the aircraft on the back. As a tradition, purchasing one is reserved for those who have flown on the aircraft. The son was calling to order one of the jackets for his father. He asked if we could overnight the jacket, which with a little research I determined we could, but it would be at a premium price. The son was adamant that price was not a factor.

I asked about the flight and how they all enjoyed it. His son said how special the flight was for him and the rest of them as well. He told me that since they were from all over, they decided to spend the whole day together. That evening they went out to dinner, and the veteran explained that after each mission his crew would get together and take a shot of whiskey. To keep with that tradition, at dinner they did the same. Then their father pulled a small notebook from his pocket where he kept his notes from his missions. This notebook had the list of targets with notes to himself like, "Lots of fighters or flak," and others to that affect. On this day he wrote, "Mission number 36, I flew with my family today." The son continued to tell me that after dinner they went home, and that evening their father died in his sleep. The family wanted the jacket so badly because they had decided to bury him in it. That is what the B-17 meant to him. That is how he wanted history to remember him.

◀ U.S. Air Force F-15 Eagle fighter pilot Scott Taylor with his wife, Katie, who is also an F-15 pilot. After hearing stories about his grandfather's wartime service, he too wanted to fly.

◀ World War II bombardier Don Taylor. He lost his life in the skies over Europe and would never know that his legacy inspired his grandson to fly.

CHIP CULPEPPER

The reason for Chip Culpepper's interest in the B-17 is due to his father, Conley Culpepper. Conley served as a top turret gunner and flight engineer on B-17s during World War II. He was assigned to the "Bloody 100th" Bomb Group, 349th Bomb Squadron, based at RAF Thorpe Abbotts. Conley flew 35 missions and then returned home to Arkansas.

If any photo is worth the proverbial thousand words, it would be the one Chip Culpepper shared with us after a flight in our B-17 *Aluminum Overcast*, a photo that was more than 70 years in the making. It depicted Chip holding a photo of his father's B-17 crew in front of our aircraft after his flight. A perfect balance of past and future.

"My father and I went out to see a visiting B-17 in the 1990s," Chip said. "At that time, there were still a good amount of WWII veterans left, and a few of them had gathered near the aircraft. When [Dad] walked up, one of them identified him as a B-17 veteran and asked him his unit. My father replied, '100th Bomb Group.' They all just rather took a step back, and one of them said, 'We didn't think there were any of you guys still around.'" Chip said he was worried about his father being able to move through the airplane, but quickly realized he didn't need to be concerned.

"I remember when my dad approached the airplane, he ran his hands down the prop and along a rivet line, almost as if he was shaking hands with an old friend," Chip said. "I was worried about dad's mobility to get into the airplane and crawl on his hands and knees through it due to his arthritis. Little did I know that I would find myself struggling to keep up with him. Once inside it was almost as if his muscle memory made him decades younger. He climbed into his old turret again and took a few moments. Each time he would touch a different part of the plane he would have another story. Stories that I had never heard before. It is almost as if the plane was giving them permission to let the stories out."

Months later, Conley took part in the 100th Bomb Group reunion — the only one he ever attended before he died in 2000.

In 1995, Chip thought he would surprise his father with a B-17 ride. After consulting his wife, he bought the ticket and called his dad to surprise him.

"I called him and said, 'What are you up to? I bought you a ticket on this B-17,'" Chip said. "The phone was silent for a few moments. My father said, 'I've done it. I want you to go and tell me about your flight.'" What he had planned as a surprise for his father was about to turn into a massive history lesson for Chip.

"To fly in the same type of aircraft that my father served in was an experience that is hard to put into words," Chip said. "I can remember sitting there in the back waiting for startup. It was powerful to see the startup and smoke coming out of the engines on startup. I had a very small view of what his life was like during the war."

In 2018, *Aluminum Overcast* returned to Chip's town. There was a call out for any veterans to be a part of the tour stop. "We found Paul Calkin and knew we had to take him up," Chip said. "Paul flew in the 100th Bomb Group like Dad. In February of 1943, his aircraft was damaged, and they had to ditch in the North Sea. Luckily for them, there was a Royal Air Force rescue boat nearby that was able to pick them up."

Thanks to Chip, and the local EAA chapter, Paul once again flew in a B-17. The last time he was in one was during the war. The tour stop took a unique turn for the Culpepper family home as well. Chip wanted to take his son and daughter up for a flight to experience what their grandfather had.

"At the last minute my wife decided she, too, would join us," Chip said. "My entire family was together flying in honor of Dad. My son is named after Dad and on the day of our flight was the same age as my father was when he was flying his missions: 19 years old. The flight would also take place 70 years to the day of Conley's first combat mission. My daughter wore his dog tags and smiled the entire flight."

Though Conley has gone west, his memory and legacy continue to inspire others through the efforts of his family. Conley Culpepper III has since been accepted into officer training in the U.S. Marine Corps where he hopes to become an aviator.

◄ Anna and Conley Culpepper III holding a photo of their grandfather on the day of their flight.

CLOSING

I CLOSE THIS BOOK just as I began it, sitting with the B-17 in the **Kermit Weeks** Hangar. Sitting back in the waist section of the aircraft I am surrounded by the sounds, feel, and smells of the aircraft that helped bring alive the memories of those whose lives were entwined with the B-17. I didn't plan the journey that I went on with this aircraft, but I am forever thankful that it happened. I am thankful not just for the knowledge and lessons I gained from the veterans themselves, but also for the relationships I have built with their families. Our *Aluminum Overcast* continues to travel the country and spread the word about the men and women who are associated with the B-17. Our volunteers who crew the aircraft are truly dedicated to the mission of making sure these stories continue into the future.

I have been fortunate enough to have traveled around the Midwest talking about the legacy of the B-17. Through doing this, I have had the chance to meet even more veterans and share in their stories. There are two talks that will always remain special for me. The first was at the National Museum of the Mighty Eighth Air Force in Savannah, Georgia, the birthplace of the group that would deploy the B-17 so effectively in Europe. The other was at the National Museum of the United States Air Force in Dayton, Ohio, for the dedication of the restored B-17 *Memphis Belle*. This was special for me as the *Belle* was one of the aircraft that as a kid first sparked my interest in the B-17 and in aviation in general. The chance to speak at the dedication of this aircraft is a moment I will forever hold special. The talks I give are my way of educating and inspiring young folks to take the next step and read more about our heroes. I like to think we are doing our part to tell the story of a brave generation and what this one special airplane means to so many people. I consider it our highest honor.

Chris Henry

MORE THAN 75 YEARS AGO, a bunch of teenagers and young twentysomethings put it all on the line to save the world. The opportunity to help Chris share some of their remarkable stories in this book was a project I couldn't wait to take on. The title page says "Chris Henry with Hal Bryan," but it really shouldn't. It should say "Chris Henry with EAA." I accept the nod as co-author with some flavor of begrudging grace, and only on behalf of an extraordinarily passionate and dedicated team, all of whom worked tirelessly through nights and weekends to help shape the book you hold in your hands right now.

This experience has been unforgettable, and it was my humble privilege to have made a modest contribution to such a worthwhile endeavor. We can never forget the service nor, especially, the sacrifice of those men and women who stepped up decades before we were born, in so many cases trading their lives for the ones we enjoy now. If this book causes even one reader to pause and reflect, to look back at the boys of the Flying Fortresses — and the girls who built and ferried them — and feel the profound gratitude that Chris and I share with all of our colleagues at EAA, then we will have accomplished our mission.

Hal Bryan

ACKNOWLEDGMENTS

FOR MY WIFE, KAREN — WITHOUT YOUR SUPPORT, I'D NEVER GET OFF THE GROUND.

Just like crewing a B-17 on a mission, this book took an entire team of people. Their hard work, skills, and talents are what has truly made this project come to fruition. What made the journey even more fun was doing this book with those who became friends. The book has been developed over years of research and interviews collected in conjunction with EAA's B-17 Flight Experience program. There are countless people to thank. First and foremost, thank you to the veterans who flew or served aboard the B-17. Without you, our world would forever be different. Thank you for sharing your stories, both good and bad, to help paint an accurate picture of life in a bomber. Thank you to the families who shared their stories, photos, and most importantly, their family's legacy. It is my hope that younger generations of these families are able to read this book and discover just how amazing their grandparents and great-grandparents were.

Thank you to Jack and Rose Pelton who first believed in this project of mine and pushed me to create a book about it. To Jim Busha, whom I turned to many times for guidance and direction. This book would not have been possible without him. Thank you to Col. Frank Borman for the fantastic honor of the wonderful foreword, his support, and friendship. Thanks to Dr. Harry Friedman for the heartfelt foreword as well as his inspiration and friendship. A very special thank-you to Dr. Bill Harrison. Without him, we would not have our B-17, and these veterans would have never had the experiences with us that they did.

Thank you to EAA's editorial team of Hal Bryan, Colleen Walsh, Ti Windisch, Jen Knaack, and Sam Oleson, who worked hard to ensure that the single giant sentence I gave them was sculpted properly into a coherent book humans could understand. To Kayla Floyd, who has spent hours with me, writing captions for stacks of black-and-white photos, and for coordinating the production of the entire thing. To Brandon Jacobs, who has created a beautiful layout to take readers on this journey, and to Sara Nisler, Alden Frautschy, and Amber Pawlitzke for helping it come to life in the digital realm. Thank you to Connor Madison for his gorgeous current-day photos, which appear in this book and bring the crew stations to life, as well as the amazing cover. To Christina Basken for her beautiful photos as well. Thanks to Lily Johnson for her support and input. Thanks to Max Platts and Tom Charpentier for always pushing me to dig deeper and learn more, and for coming with me on this adventure. This would have been nowhere near as fun without you.

Thank you to Kristy Busse and Olivia Rasmus. Without you not only would we not leave the ground, but we would have never flown any of our veterans. Thank you to Brittany Farrell, Nicole Paris, Emily Grubbs, and Courtney Hayes for trusting me with your media flights and enabling this airplane to be shared with so many veterans. A sincere thank-you to the veterans and families of

Peter Hill, Ed Hudson, Henning Elsasser, Eugene Benedetti, Janis Benedetti Fitzsimmons, Hewitt T. "Shorty" Wheless, Hal Weekley, Donald Christensen, Edwin Davidson, Thomas Hardin, Howard Krasemann, Pat Patterson, Robert Killmark, Ed Stevens, Donald W. Stoulil, James Clem, Clint Hammond, Richard Gillespie, John Corcoran, Jim Stopulos, Chuck Childs, Connie Childs Peterson, William H. Long, Doug Holt, John "Lucky" Luckadoo, Everett Phillips, Robert Schneider, Floyd Hendershot, Bob Spraight, Donald Muston, Robert Burkart, George E. Freitag, Frank Gramenzi, Loran Heeb, Mirwood Starkey, Harvin Abrahamson, Alan Chandler and Fern Bridges, Ray Miner, Daniel Blitz, Donald Camp, Dean Larson, Earl Service, Charles E. Lynn, Howard Bobb, John and Jo Tarabula, Cindy Tarabula Post, Fred and Betty Zurbuchen, Doug Ward and Judie Ohm, Oscar W. Krigbaum, Roy O'Neil, Jack Dempsey Robertson, Calvin G. Turkington, Jack Dodson, Jack Wallace, June Morris, Betty Lausch, Catherine Jones, Betty Strohfus, Blanche Gangwere, Robert Gangwere, Chip Culpepper, and Conley Culpepper.

I want to extend a personal thank-you to my friends and family. Even though they did not always understand what it was that I was working on, they showed me their support in any way they could to help inspire me. To my wife, Karen, my rock. I am so thankful that you are my partner, love of my life, and best friend. I couldn't do any of this without you. To my daughter, Elizabeth, who has taught me that it is cool to still be a kid. To my mom and dad, Patty and Don Henry, for giving me everything I needed to to succeed, from a ride to the airport to going to college. My grandparents, Patsy and Maria Bevilacqua, who always blew me away with their stories of evading the Nazis in World War II and hiding Allied flyers in their basements and woods. For anyone reading this, your grandparents are way cooler than you will ever realize. Trust me. To Fernando "Zizi" Bevilacqua, my uncle, who is to blame for my love of everything from muscle cars to airplanes, who would always bring me magazines and books featuring WWII airplanes. My aunt, Pam Bevilacqua, who, no matter the life event, was right there in the front row, holding the camera. To my Grandma Henry, I will always remember you tearing Beaver County apart looking for a specific model of the B-17 for me. To Tim and Jennifer Rodriguez, I am not even sure where to begin. I am lucky to have you both in my life. Your friendship crossed the line from friends to family years ago. To the guys and gals of Air Heritage, the first stop on my path to airplanes. Thank you for giving me such a wonderful foundation. Thank you for taking the time to share your knowledge and time with a 12-year-old kid. Thanks to Bob Huddock for always having the time to go flying and talk about the future. Thank you to Tom Walton who inspired my imagination through model aviation. Thanks to Rob and Bob Morelli for showing me that aircraft restoration is an art form. To Clair Pazey and the Pazey family; the whole time I knew Clair, I thought he was teaching me about airplanes, but he was actually teaching me about life. I will be forever thankful for my time with him.

Last but not least, I want to thank everyone I have been on staff with at EAA. It is such an honor to get to work next to all of you. I have never been a part of such a dedicated and hardworking team. It is truly a privilege.

CREDITS